Bewitch ...

To truly enchant and bewitch a loved one, enter his or her dreams using nutmeg, a crystal, a feather, a silk scarf, and Star Anise.

Bother ...

Unhex a wicked mirror that makes you look less-than-sexy using apple cider, vinegar, ammonia, and white magnolia soap while chanting the secret chant revealed within.

Bewilder ...

Your lover will never leave you once you've conjured up the sensual, edible Elixir of Bliss from jasmine rice, rose flower water, sweet coconut milk, white cardamom seeds, and curry.

With this wickedly romantic guide, you need never again be
bewildered about the mysteries of love.

Also by Lexa Roséan

THE SUPERMARKET SORCERESS

The Supermarket Sorceress's
Sexy Hexes

Lexa Roséan

St. Martin's Paperbacks

For Fatima, and all the gods and
goddesses of laughter, lust,
and love.

NOTE TO READER

While the spells and enchantments which follow use commonly available ingredients, if you have any allergies or sensitivities to a particular ingredient, refrain from attempting that spell. Heed all warnings and instructions on the products you use.

CONTENTS

SECTION III: LOVE AND GLAMOUR

SECTION IV: BATHING BEAUTIES AND SHOWER POWER

SECTION V: LOVE TALK

SECTION VI: LOVE ON THE ROCKS

SECTION VII: TROUBLESHOOTING AND TECHNICALITIES

SECTION VIII: BEES' KNEES—A Whole Lot of Honey Spells

SECTION IX: SOUL MATES

SECTION X: LONGEVITY AND PROTECTION

SECTION XI: TRIPLE XXX HEXES AND XTRA ADDED LOVE

SECTION XII: LOVE AND THE LAW

SECTION XIII: LOVE, MELANCHOLIA, MAD CRUSHES, FIXATIONS, OBSESSIVE BEHAVIOR, AND BORDERLINE STALKING

SECTION XIV: LOVE CURES

INTRODUCTION

Greetings, all who have been anxiously awaiting this book. The Supermarket Sorceress, alias Sexy Lexy, Lexa de Hexa, or Lady Venus (as I am known in witch circles), returns with over *soixante-neuf* spells, charms, and enchantments for love, lust, and other a*sordid* situations. As a high priestess and witch since 1982, I have counseled people from all walks of life who have come to me with troubles in love. I have kept a *grimoire* on all successful spells composed by myself as well as those shared by other wonderful witches. This book is based on that work. Because many traditional spells contain very difficult-to-obtain items, I have designed the spells in this book to work with items you can obtain in your local supermarket or hardware store. Do not think for a moment that these ingredients are less powerful than the traditional ones. According to the principles of pantheism, there is a life force or divine spark within everything found upon the earth. Witches themselves believe that rocks or stones (especially those tumbled in the ocean) contain very magical properties. Why should a poultry lacer be any less powerful than a sword, provided it's been properly consecrated? So do not underestimate the power of a black dishrag!

Some commonly asked questions are What is magic? Do spells work? How do they work? Magic is creative ritual, desire made manifest. Magic is prayer. A spell is a form of magic, therefore a form of prayer. Not all spells work. Some prayers go unanswered. A spell may not work because of a variety of reasons. The gods may be too busy at such time to answer your call. You may not have put enough energy into the spell. You may be asking for something you don't really need. The ingredients in the spell may not be in tune with your aura.

Spells work because they trigger subconscious energy locked within your own brain. You are one magical component. The second component is the energy in the ingredients themselves. Spells unlock your own subconscious power and blend it with the power of nature.

Love spells in particular are the most popular type of spell. There are two rules of thumb that apply to love magic:

1. Do what ye will and harm none.
2. All's fair in love and war.

Do I contradict myself? Very well then I contradict myself.... I contain multitudes. (Thank you, Walt Whitman.)

Choose the rule that applies to you or the rule that applies to you in a particular situation. Or mix and match as you will.

As the popular old song implies, most love spells, no matter how well you weave them, are considered black magic. That is because these spells are designed to bend the will of another. Spells to heal the heart, spells to attract loving or lustful *energy* (as opposed to a *specific person's energy*), are not considered black magic.

It is interesting to observe the progression of love spells throughout the centuries. Compare, if you will, an ancient Coptic spell

> *May so and so pant like a bitch in heat over his/her desire for me.*
> *May he/she have no happiness, no peace, no sleep,*
> *no appetite, only hunger and lust for me.*
> *Do not let the soul of so and so rest until he/she comes to me.*

with a New Age love prayer:

> *Divine power, may my husband cheat or*
> *not cheat on me, all according to Your will.*

Honestly, we move from the completely demonic to the namby-pamby of magical intent. I have tried to find a middle ground with these spells. Use all at your own risk. Choose a spell designed to suit your conscience. There is, by the way, a witch's saying: "You lose them the way you get them." So all who are about to venture into the spell land of "I want who's not mine," please keep this in mind.

Pick a spell that attracts you. You will notice and therefore ask: "Lady Venus, why are there three different spells for love attraction? Which one is the right one?" There are many roads, or rather, all roads lead to Mecca. There are over a thousand love attraction spells, and that is because each spell does not work for every individual. Think of antibiotics. Your doctor may choose from several hundred; the trick is to find the one your system will respond to. The same principle applies to magical ingredients. Follow your own intuition. If a spell does not work for you, try a different approach. You have to find the spell that speaks to your soul. What works for Vladimir may not work for Alexander.

You may also ask: "If vanilla whets the sexual appetite, how can it also create harmony with relatives? If one nut helps you please your lover, how can many nuts cure sexual deviancy?" The explanation for this is what I call "the water principle." Every ingredient has a property. The combination of specific quantities of two ingredients creates a third energy or property. Hydrogen and oxygen are both gases. When we mix two parts hydrogen to one part oxygen, the liquid H_2O is formed. If we mix two parts hydrogen to two parts oxygen, we get H_2O_2, hydrogen peroxide. Its properties are very different from those of water. Hydrogen combined with chloride becomes a corrosive acid. Think "chemistry" when you mix your potions.

At this point I know you are thinking: C'mon, Glenda, get on with it!

All right, then. Hold on to your ruby slippers, 'cuz here we go. I hope this book brings a lot of love and a lot of laughs into your life.

Blessed Be ✪
Lexa Roséan (aka Lady Venus)
NYC 1997

Acknowledgments (and heartfelt thanks) to

The writers room
The ever magical and inspirational Dorjanda
The Great American in Liberty
Key Food of Avenue A
C-Town of Avenue D
Arbeter Ring Bookstore
R. N. Schachter, painter of saints
Scholar and siren Carolyn Shapiro
Joni YOGAcalsik
Donna Binder
The Hirshorn pen and the Hirshorn Living French
    Dictionary
Golebiowski & Szczudlo, most handsome, most helpful,
    and couple voted most likely to succeed
Kath ''the shagger'' Burlinson
26.6 in under 4 chef H. Griffiths
The unsinkable Fräulein Brown
The Rebbitzen, Raisel the Royta, Frog, and Tad
Lady Miw, Eroh, Lord Jupiter, Silversnake, Apollo, Edwin,
    Bejornkin, and Enchantments
Jennifer Enderlin
S. Martin, master of the deal or contract mistress
La Perichole Kishka and Piquillo Broadway, my loving
    ''mewses''

Frauka, Carina, and *l'école du Teddy Bear Tango* for re-
awakening my passion, drama, and joie de vivre.
Garbo 180
Claire O! ''my bubbie'' Moed

BY THE LIGHT OF THE SILVERY MOON

Witches consider the moon the divine light of the goddess. It is important to follow her signals when casting spells. There are three basic aspects of the moon: *dark, new,* and *full.* These aspects are divided into two phases known as *waxing* and *waning* moons. The waxing moon happens from new to full, as the moon's light increases. The waning moon period is from two days after full until new. During this time the moon's light decreases. During a waning or dark moon it is customary to do cleansing and healing magic and to get rid of obstacles in a relationship. During a waxing period, magic can be done to attract, draw, and enhance the positive. A new moon is best for young love or to attract someone new. Full moons are best for fleshing out and culminating your desires. The best magic is begun on a new moon and continued into the full moon. If you can keep your focus for a new to full moon phase, your magical results will reflect your efforts.

Your local newspaper should give new and full moon times and dates in the weather box. For a more in-depth look at the moon, I suggest obtaining an ephemeris or astrological calendar. My personal favorite is *Jim Maynard's Pocket Astrologer.* This way you will know not only the phase of the moon, but what sign it is in. The following is a suggested list or guideline of love magic themes for the twelve zodiac signs. Remember as well, regardless of the guidelines, if the moon is in your sun sign or in the sun sign of your lover, this is considered a personal best day for you and your magic.

Moon in Aries

This is the "next to lovin', I like fightin' best" moon, so be careful about how much magical heat you create on an Aries moon. You don't want to end up quarreling instead of kissing. Moon in Aries is about taking initiative in love, for yourself or to promote someone else to make the first move (see "Chased Spell"). This is also the best moon for the impatient magician. Aries moon will bring quick results. Waning: can be utilized to banish impatience and/or anger.

Moon in Taurus

The *Xanadu* moon. Sensuality, security. The one moon where love and money mix. Waning: can be used to banish codependency and jealousy.

Moon in Gemini

The *love talk* moon. Focus on communication and flirtation. Also the best time to do magic where triangle situations are involved. Waning: writing Dear John letters, figuring how to deliver the breaking-up news.

Moon in Cancer

The *bathing beauty* moon. Protecting home, family, children. During a waning Cancer moon you can banish moodiness.

Moon in Leo

Self-love, sexual prowess, creative lovemaking (see "Sunlight Spell for Sexual Energy"). Waning: banish ego and false pride, shame.

Moon in Virgo

Technicalities moon. Sexual health, emotional health, discrimination in choosing partners. Waning: getting rid of bad habits or baggage in relationships.

Moon in Libra

Love and the law moon. Focus on partnerships and soul mates. Waning: justice; taking a partner from someone (bad karma).

Moon in Scorpio

Emphasis on sex, sex, sex (see "Sex, Lust, and Other aSORDID Spells"). Waning moon in Scorpio is perfect for revenge! The high road would be sexual healing or getting rid of negative sexual behavior.

Moon in Sagittarius

Meeting a tall dark stranger. Second honeymoon or love travel. Wisdom for your relationship (see "Love Cures"). Waning: banish a wandering eye in a partner or in yourself.

Moon in Capricorn

Working toward the long haul. Giving longevity to a relationship (see "Longevity and Protection"). Waning: getting rid of chronic problems in the relationship; dumping obsessiveness and stalkers (see "Love, Melancholia, Mad Crushes, Fixations, Obsessive Behavior, and Borderline Stalking").

Moon in Aquarius

Freedom. Idealism. Friendship. Love. Healing. Waning: creating emotional detachment.

Moon in Pisces

Glamour moon. Waning: get rid of deception and illusion.

The moon changes signs about every one and a half to two days. Do not let this information stifle your need to work any particular spell at any particular time (although I do suggest you follow the basic guideline of waning and waxing). Let it be an enhancement. For example, suppose you are obsessing over your relationship and it is interfering with your work. At the same time, you do not want to lose the wonderful romance that is already in progress. Do the Spell for Resolve and Action while the moon is in Virgo or Aquarius to help you detach and focus on your work. When the moon enters Pisces (hopefully that won't fall on a school night), choose a spell from the "Romance, Dating, Attraction" section. Working with the signs of the moon is kind of like eating organic produce. You go with the flow, the energy that the universe presents to you. You may be in the mood for corn, but kale is in the market. Think about what kale might do for your table (relationship). Go with it. Take the organic energy that the lunar grocer provides. It may be just what you need. Hey, it may not. In that case, do what ye will, and get yourself some frozen corn from the supermarket. Work that A'maize'n Lover Spell for all its worth!

Yet I implore the open-minded to try aligning themselves with the lunar and astrological forces. Put aside what you think you need and just ponder the kale. For instance, suppose you are happily married and the moon is waning in Capricorn. "I don't have any stalkers," you say. Okay, fair enough. But what is the one thing (even if it's only for this week) that has been bugging or stalking you about your relationship? Maybe it's the thought that it is too good to be true. Waning moon in Capricorn would be the time to get rid of that thought.

Blue moons happen once in a blue moon. A blue moon occurs when you have two full moons in the same month. The second full moon is the blue moon. Blue moons are a time for miracle magic and soul mate magic.

Void of course moons are not to be messed with. They occur when the moon is moving between two zodiac signs. It is called "void of course" because there is no specific guiding energy force aligned with the moon during this motion. Check your astrological calendar for exact times. Doing magic during a void of course moon can be treacherous.

LOVE ALTARS

A love altar is a sacred space set aside to honor the gods and goddesses of love. It is also a special place to work your love magic. Love altars can be created out of a tabletop, a nightstand, even a kitchen counter. Traditional witches include an image of god and goddess on their altars, as well as a representation of the four elements: earth, wind, fire, and water. Some witches have beautiful statues of Venus of Wilendorf or Venus de Milo on their altars. Some witches use a seashell to represent the goddess and a pinecone to represent the god. You can be creative and choose an image that represents the divine ruler of love to you. The element of earth is usually represented by salt. For a love altar, rosebuds or any love herb might be a better choice. Air is symbolized by incense. You may use a feather to bring swiftness in love. The fire element is fulfilled through a candle. Pink and red are best for love. Water is placed in a bowl upon the altar. For love altars, rosewater, spring water, or a dish of honey are the best choices.

It is also traditional to place flowers on a love altar. They should be replaced every Friday. Always keep the altar clean and change the flower water every day or every other day. It is okay to set up an altar just to work a spell and then to dismantle it afterward. Some witches prefer to have an altar set up at all times, some only when they are doing magical work.

A bell is another common object found upon the altar. I have a copper bell in the shape of an apple on my love altar. I ring it every time I need to speak to the goddess about matters of love. Any romantic image or token from a lover (a letter, a photo,*

*Never put a picture of a living person next to a burning candle. It is considered bad luck! You may place the photo on the opposite side of the altar if you wish.

a ring, and so forth) can also be placed upon the altar. You can create a small love altar on the edge of the tub as you take your honey bath. Just place a seashell, a feather, a red votive candle, and an apple or a rosebud on the ledge.

Maintaining a constant love altar will keep your home flowing with love. Setting up a love altar to do your work will lend extra power to the spell. In ancient times, the body of the priestess herself was a love altar. For all spells that involve anointing the body, treat yourself or your lover as though you were an altar of love.

What follows are some suggestions for specific types of love altars.

LOVE UNCROSSING ALTAR

You should use a white covering of linen or silk. White or pink candles and white or pink flowers (such as carnations) are especially useful in removing negative emotional energy. You may also place eggs or oval-shaped stones upon this altar. Keep a bowl of salt water on the altar as well. This altar is designed to support any spell worked to alleviate problems in a relationship or to remove obstacles from the path to finding love.

LOVE ATTRACTION ALTAR

Pink or red cloth of satin or silk, red and pink roses, or any exotic flower should be placed upon this altar. Bright copper pennies (for earth), open fans (for air), and an open jar of honey should be used instead of water.

GLAMOUR ALTAR

I would suggest old black-and-white photos of Garbo, Dietrich, and Colette, but you may have an altogether different concept of glamour in your mind. Let your imagination run wild. Cut out glamourous images from magazines and create a collage on your tabletop instead of using a cloth covering. Substitute dried mushrooms and rose petals for salt. Obtain a peacock feather if you can. Use pure beeswax candles. Instead of water on the altar, use orange blossom honey.

LOVE TALK ALTAR

This altar will support all spells in the "**Love Talk**" section. Use an orange or yellow cloth of linen or silk. Place a bowl of cinnamon powder on the altar. Use many assorted feathers (goosedown are favored). Burn orange and white candles for clear communication. Flavor the water on your altar with a few drops of cinnamon extract. Lavender flowers and pink roses should be used. Any representation of the god Hermes and the goddess Aphrodite will make this altar most effective.

LOVE AND PROTECTION ALTAR

Use a white cloth of linen or silk or a lace doily. Lavender, red or white roses, and sunflowers can all be used. Place a picture of you and your mate within a circle of salt, sage, and rosebuds. Circular and heart-shaped objects are favored to decorate the altar. Instead of a candle, obtain a small night-light and plug it into an outlet above the altar. This way your love will have a continual flame.

General Note: Just remember that an altar is a very personal aspect of magic. You must choose a place and images that feel sacred to you and are connected with the desire you hope to fulfill. Try playing mood music and dress sexy when you approach your love altar. Your love altar is the place for you to dance, sing, chant, pray,* meditate, and work your magic spell. There is no right or wrong here, only what works for you!

*Bitch to the goddess.

Magical Manners

A Simple Guide for All Magical Procedures

1. Always say "Please" and "Thank you." Gods, goddesses, and spirits respond to courtesy and appreciation.
2. Never mix love and money magic (unless you are in the sex industry).
3. Approach your spell with clarity of purpose.
4. One spell at a time works best (especially for beginners).
5. Keep your altar and magical workspace tidy. "Cleanliness is next to god(dess)liness."
6. Don't panic. Have patience in waiting for results.
7. Never perform a spell on a lunar or solar eclipse. This is the one time witches consider to be unlucky for casting spells.
8. Always dispose of your magical remnants properly when your spell has been completed. (Don't litter, recycle, and so forth.) If food is biodegradable, you may leave it outside under a tree.
9. Do not attempt to win back a lover when you are angry. Do a love healing spell first.
10. Do not perform a love attraction spell while you are experiencing low self-esteem. Do a self-love spell first.
11. Check the phase of the moon and make sure it is compatible with the spell you are working.
12. Choose a magical or sexy name when you do a love spell. My name is Lady Venus. Most witches use a god or goddess name in a magic circle to empower

their work and to remove themselves from the world of the mundane. In medieval times, the witch name was used for protection. If you and I had met to dance under the full moon and an Inquisitor caught you the next day and asked, ''Which witches did you defile yourself with?'' you of course would not want to betray your friends. But suppose the Inquisitor hung you on the rack, pried open your toenails, and poured salt and pepper on your open wounds? Suppose he beat you so senseless that you lost your mind and cried out, ''Lady Venus! I defiled myself with Lady Venus!'' That is what you would have said, as you would have known me by no other name. When the Inquisitor dialed 411 to look me up, he would have found no such listing.

Here are some suggestions for magical (or craft) names. Please feel free to be creative and make up some of your own.

GIRLS	*BOYS*
Sheba	Pan
Cleo	Dionysus
Aphrodite	Eros
Siren	Stud

13. Do what ye will and harm none.

Romance, Dating, Attraction

APPLE LOVE SPELL REVISITED

Ingredient:

  one red apple

In my first book, I mention an apple love spell. Here is a more powerful and effective version of that spell. We are essentially going to combine two rituals. The first is the removal of the apple stem. Twist the stem of an apple. On each rotation call out a letter of the alphabet. Begin with A. The letter you call out as the stem comes off the apple will be the initial of your true love. Of course, you can trust your luck and blessings and completely leave it up to fate which letter the old stem parts from the apple on. If it parts on the initial of the person you desire, rest assured that this love is destined. If you do not trust your luck, you can purposely pull the stem on a particular letter. (This is called using your will.)

Once you have pulled the stem from the apple, hold it between your teeth and make a wish to be with that particular person. If you have willed the letter, you obviously have someone in mind. If you have pulled a random letter—say, S—ask the goddess to bring this S to you.

The second part of this spell can be performed only when you have a particular person in mind, unless you are ready to randomly offer half an apple to every person you meet whose name begins with the letter *S*. According to Gypsy myth, the apple represents the heart. If you cut the apple in half horizontally, you will reveal the pentacle: sacred symbol of the goddess and the human form (head, two arms, two legs, forming the five points). The Gypsy lovers would share these two apple halves, symbolically giving each other their hearts.

You will offer half of the stem-plucked apple to the one you desire. If it is accepted, his or her heart will be open to your magic. However, a kiss must occur within thirteen hours after the eating of the apple. If you initiate the kiss, you have a good shot at winning your beloved's affections. If the other person initiates the kiss, you have already won his or her heart. If the kiss is mutual, the bond will last.

LOVE DRAWING SPELL

Ingredients:

paper sipping straw

In order to bewitch someone, it is quite useful as well as traditional to collect some piece of the person so that you can create a sympathetic link. Hair, nails, the person's signature on paper, and saliva are all good possessions to work effective spells. This spell combines the luminescence of the goddess with the magical link of your intended.

An easy and sexy way to collect a bodily link with someone you want to attract is to steal a straw they have sucked upon. Carefully wrap the straw in plastic wrap and save it until the full moon. At such time you will hold the straw with the end that was touched by their lips up to the light of the moon. Use the straw as a telescope to view the powerful orb of the Great Mother. Then place your mouth upon the unused end of the straw. Suck air through it and imagine the full light of the moon illuminating this relationship. Visualize the two of you kissing under the full moon. Ask the goddess to kiss and bless and anoint your lips in order to receive each other. Bend the straw in half and insert the other end between your lips. Bite down on both ends, binding what has touched his or her wet mouth to what has touched your wet mouth.

Remove the straw ends from your mouth and insert one end into the other to create union. Set the straw on fire to create desire. Bury the ashes so that the magic can be grounded and therefore made manifest.

Warning: Do not forget which end your desired one sucked upon or you will not perform this spell correctly. If the end that touched his or her lips touches your lips, before it has been blessed by the light of the moon, this person will be repelled by the sight of you.

Precautionary Note: If you do not want anyone to work this spell on you, always break your straw in half when you are done with it. The spell is effective only when performed with a whole straw.

Secret Tip: This spell is most effective when sarsaparilla has been sipped through the straw. Sarsaparilla is used for love and happiness and is alleged to make wishes come true.

SPELL TO CAUSE ANOTHER TO FALL IN LOVE WITH YOU

Ingredients:

    three strands of corn silk
    three hairs from your own head
    olive oil
    red wine or red fruit juice
    a jar
    red string
    matches

red marker pen
corn husk

This spell is based on a modified version of an old Sicilian love spell. On a Friday evening at midnight, on or close to the new moon (the first Friday after the new moon), pluck three hairs from your head. Entwine them with three strands of corn silk. Chant the following:

Weaver of silk weaver of time weaver of fate weaver of rhyme Entwine my fate with _____.
May (he or she) wrap close to me in heart, in mind, in body, in soul. May he or she have no rest until joined with me we are whole.
As I will so mote it be.

Roll the hair and corn silk round and round in the palms of your hands until your hands are well heated. Stretch a dried corn husk out flat and with a red marker draw a heart. Write the name of your intended inside the heart. Write your name inside the lines of an arrow and let the arrow pierce the heart. Now place the hair and corn silk inside the husk and roll it up tight. Tie the husk with a red string you have anointed with your own saliva. Simply take the string and run it softly between your moist lips. Touch the rolled parchment to your heart and then place it in a safe vessel and set it on fire. As it burns, visualize your intended's heart burning for you. Let the scroll burn completely, then gather the ashes and place them in a bottle or jar of olive oil. Hide the jar beneath your bed until the full moon. On the full moon you must dip your left thumb into the oil and wipe the rim of a glass containing red wine or red fruit juice. Serve to your intended.

This spell is very effective and known to work immediately. I advise you to use it with caution.

FRIENDSHIP SPELL

Ingredients:

> **tangerines**
> **pumpkin seeds**
> **sunflower seeds**
> **Brazil nuts**
> **carob**
> **apricot**

Romance is great, but friends are there to help pick up the pieces when a relationship falls apart. Some people never count on lovers but always count on friends. This spell can be used to attract new and true friends or to deepen the bonds of existing friendships. You can use the Love Healing Bath to heal a friendship that is in trouble.

Although some of these ingredients are considered foods of passion, they evoke passion from the heart. Tangerines have similar qualities to oranges, yet they are more playful and do not represent a monogamous relationship as oranges do. Pumpkin seeds are considered the children of Oshun, the Yoruban love goddess. They can help you create a family of friends. Sunflower seeds represent truth and loyalty when mixed with other nuts. Brazil nuts are ruled by Gemini, the sign of communication, and Aquarius, the sign of friendship. Carob is ruled by Venus and is used for nonsexual love. Apricots are associated with love and longevity and can help you keep your friends for life. Lay out a large bowl of these foods and munch on them with your friends to deepen the bonds between you. Eat on your own to attract true and loyal friends.

CHASTE SPELL

Ingredients:

> **sage**
> **white flour**
> **onion powder**

Dust your whole body down with sage, white flour, and onion powder before a date. These purifying agents will keep your sex drive in check and keep you chaste.

These ingredients can cool down overamorous minors. Sometimes the hormones develop faster than the heart and the mind. It is important to give them time to catch up. This spell is excellent for teenagers, who really should wait before becoming sexually active. It helps to promote abstinence and to develop patience in matters of the heart to combat the instant-gratification society we live in.

CHASED SPELL

Ingredients:

> **white talcum powder (unscented)**
> **capful of rum or imitation rum extract**
> **crushed bay leaves**
> **dried and crushed basil leaves**
> **thyme**
> **piece of an aloe leaf or aloe vera juice**
> **red and orange gelatin powder**

These ingredients are a modified version of a traditional recipe called Mount Powder.* Its origins are unknown. Mount powder is said to increase your sexual stamina and allure. By adding gelatin, which contains marrow from horses' hooves, we can create a game of pursuit. Pour a half cup of talcum powder into a bowl. Slowly add twenty drops of rum or rum extract. Put in a pinch of each: bay, basil, and thyme. Squeeze in a drop of aloe vera juice or a snip of the leaf. Add a half teaspoon each of red and orange gelatin powder. (Red is the color of lust and orange the color of the hunt. Together they create excitement and movement.) Mix well and dust your arms and legs. Do this after showering and before dressing. This lustful mixture will increase your sexual magnetism and assure that you are constantly chased.

SELF-LOVE SPELL

Ingredients:

> **mirror**
> **bowl of water**
> **a flower**

Self-love is the first step to achieving love with a partner. If we do not love and adore ourselves, how can we expect another to love and adore us? The classical Greek myth of Narcissus teaches us that self-love or same-sex love is sinful. Narcissus was cold-hearted and spurned the love of the nymph Echo. Aphrodite caused him to fall in love with his own reflection in the water, and he died of starvation, glued to the pool.

*Recipe from *The Magickal Formulary,* a compilation of spell formulas edited by Herman Slater. Slater, Herman (ed.). *The Magickal Formulary.* New York: Magickal Childe Inc., 1981.

Perhaps Narcissus just wanted to love himself for a while. Maybe he wanted to fall in love with someone who looked more like himself.

If you want to create more self-love, use a mirror for this spell. If you want to attract someone of the same sex, use a bowl of water with a rose floating in it. Gaze at your reflection in the bowl or mirror and whisper sweet nothings to yourself. Take the fragrant flower, dip it in the water or brush it across the mirror, and then anoint your brow. Chant: "Love's reflection come to me. As I will, so mote it be."

CHICKEN HEART LOVE SPELL

Ingredients:

raw chicken hearts
chicken livers
chicken fat
onions

This spell is for those of you who feel disappointed at reading that carrots, basil, and tomatoes can be used in a love spell. You had something meatier in mind. Chicken hearts, blood, fat, liver, and gizzard were all used in Slavic and Polish folk magic during the Middle Ages. This spell is guaranteed to be just as effective as medieval ingredients such as ground toad and powdered moles.

Chicken hearts are used to make yourself more attractive to the opposite sex. One common form of use was to rub the raw meat all over the body before going out to meet someone. It was believed to draw potential lovers. You can also grill the hearts and burn them until they are scorched, then scrape them with a knife to collect ash. Swallow this ash or mix it into the food or drink of the desired party. (Please do not perform this spell on vegetarians. It would be bad karma and would probably backfire on you.)

Chicken livers can also be used for love spells. Carve the names of great lovers into the raw livers. (Some suggestions: Caesar and Cleopatra, Anthony and Cleopatra, Romeo and Juliet, David and Jonathan, Vita and Virginia, Gertrude and Alice, Burton and Taylor, Gable and Lombard, Simba and Nala.) Choose lovers who inspire you or whom you wish to emulate. After carving, coat the livers with a fine film of olive oil. Grill for ten minutes. Imagine your romantic duo as the liver grills. Next sauté some onions to increase desire and sexual stamina. Grind and chop the liver and mix with the sautéed onions. To top it off, mix in some schmaltz (chicken fat). Chicken fat, although very high in calories and somewhat excessive, has the magical properties of attracting someone and then making them stick to you. Just as fat sticks to your ribs (bones), so shall your love stick to you. To crack the most resistant subject, smear a little of this chopped liver on a cracker and serve.

DATING SPELL

Ingredients:

> **dates**
> **powdered sugar**
> **maple syrup or honey**
> **tinfoil**

This spell is to be used to remove obstacles from getting a date. The obstacles may vary. For instance, one person may be able to make dates, but the dates don't show up or cancel out at the last minute. Another person may not be able to get a date at all. A third person may be getting dates over and over again with the wrong types. No matter what your dating obstacle, this is the spell for you.

Dates (meaning the food) are sweet and sticky and therefore attract love. They are also a food of protection and spiritual cleansing. Here is how to work the spell. Place a date in the middle of a table. With a small penknife carve your name or your initials into it. Now we must deal with the obstacles in your path. Sprinkle a circle of powdered sugar around the date. With your finger, write the obstacles into the powdered sugar (examples: "Ingrid keeps canceling" or "Low-life jerks who keep asking me out" or "No one will go out with me"). We use powdered or confectioners' sugar to represent negative obstacles that seem to stick to you, because it is a processed food and therefore has less staying power. It is also quite easy to blow away. Once you have written all your obstacles in the powdered sugar, take a deep breath and huff and puff and blow the powder away. You may want to do this ritual outside on a picnic table. You could also do it on the kitchen counter so that you can blow the sugar into the sink, or you could actually do it in the sink to avoid making a mess.

Using maple syrup or honey in a squirt bottle, spell out one to three qualities or people or situations you would like to draw into your romantic life. Spell it out on a piece of tinfoil. Pick up your date and roll it around in the maple syrup or honey until you have smothered all the words and essentially gathered them up into the date. Last but not least, eat the date. Pop it in your mouth, and as you roll it across your tongue, visualize all your dating dreams coming true!

SPELL FOR BRUCE AND MARY

Ingredients:

> **honey mustard**
> **spinach**
> **blackstrap molasses**

I was taking my two A.M. stroll for inspiration down aisle five when I ran into my gym instructor, Bruce. He was looking very dapper yet very down.

"*Qué pasa,* Bruce?" I asked.

"Oh, it goes like hell. I've been out clubbing all night and I completely struck out," said Bruce. "What does a fella have to do to get lucky in this town?"

"Bruce, how vulgar! No wonder you couldn't pick anyone up. Here, eat some of this," I said, opening a jar of honey mustard. "Alleged to introduce the attributes of chivalry to even the worst of brutes."

Bruce stuck his pinky in the jar and put a tad of honey mustard under his tongue. "Thanks, I can use all the help I can get. I don't know, lately all this he-man stuff is striking out big time. How can I become more of the strong, silent type? Those guys were scoring all night long."

I snipped a few spinach leaves off the produce rack and popped them in his mouth. "Well, here's the strong. I'm not sure how to do silent. Let's see, there's masking tape in aisle seven—"

"Oh yeah," interrupted Bruce. "It's on sale next to the assorted nuts and bolts, which are only $1.69 a—"

"Bruce, will you shut up? Let a witch think, for goddess's sake! Oh, I know. Let's use some blackstrap molasses. It's very Scorpionic. Scorpios know how to be secretive and silent, and they're sexy besides."

Bruce ran ahead of me to aisle four, grabbed a large jar of blackstrap molasses, twisted it open, and dropped a large dollop in his mouth. He puckered up his face and scowled.

"Bruce dear, that needs to go in your pocket. Kind of as a talisman for good luck and good behavior." I smiled. I reached over and picked a small jar off the shelf and handed it to him.

He wiped his mouth sheepishly and placed the small jar in his pocket. No sooner had he done so than my friend Mary rounded the corner from the candy aisle. She was holding a six-pack of mint gum and a roll of assorted fruit-filled candies, and she looked stunning in a Dior knock-off silver-sequined gown. She also wore six-inch stiletto heels and a face full o' MAC.*

"Oh, my God, is it still the witching hour?" shouted Mary. She was very bold— in fact, two-thirds of our neighborhood swore up and down that Mary was the true

---

*Very glamorous makeup not (yet) available in supermarkets.

reincarnation of Mae West. (Mae West died in 1980. Mary was born in 1971. Thus, if this is true, one of them was walking around without a soul for the last nine years. In my professional opinion, it is more likely that Mary has been possessed by the spirit of Mae West.)

Noticing Bruce behind me, she asked, "And who is this delicious man?"

Bruce did not respond—less out of demureness and more out of having molasses stuck to his teeth. I made the introductions.

"Bruce, this is Mary. Mary, Bruce."

"Well, Bruce, it's enchanting to meet you. I just popped in for a quick fix to bewitch. You see, I've been out in the clubs all night and I completely struck out. What does it take for a doll to get lucky in this town? I mean, there were a few pushy guys who tried to hit on me, but I'm after more of the strong, silent type. Y'know what I mean, Bruce?" she said, entwining her arm in his. "I think there's an after-hours club down in the meat market. We could have one drink and a dance or two, but then I would insist you take these tired little tootsies home."

Bruce nodded, flashing some pearls. He no longer cared about the molasses still sticking to his teeth. For him, a picky Virgo by nature, that meant *love!*

Mary flicked a look over her shoulder while paying for her products and called out: "Thanks, Witchy-poo. I owe you one."

"Forget it, Mary, this one's on the house. Bruce, I'll see you in church* on Sunday," I called out. But I do not believe he heard me.

Mary's voice bantered on through the automatic doors: "Oh, what developed forearms you have. And what's that in your pocket, dear? Are you a kleptomaniac or just happy to meet me?"

I saw Bruce make a beeline in the direction of his apartment.

Smiling, I paid for the opened honey mustard, spinach, and the two jars of molasses and went home to record another successful spell in my *grimoire.***

*The gym.
**Special book where witches record their magic spells.

Sex, Lust, and other a SORDID Spells

SUNLIGHT SPELL FOR SEXUAL ENERGY

Ingredients:

> **fruit**
> **sunlight**

Sunlight is amazingly invigorating. There are three parts to the sun's energy. Early morning sun is refreshing and energizing. Midafternoon sun can be draining; it's called the toxic or poison sun. The late afternoon rays are the healing sun. Of course, you cannot ingest sunlight, although you can absorb it into the body. This spell involves ingesting sun-kissed fruit or feeding it to the one you love. The spell is best worked in summer but can be done in any season as long as there is sunlight. Place the fruit (apple, pear, peach, orange) in direct sunlight. It is best to place it outside, but on a windowsill is fine. Let the fruit charge in the sunlight for at least twenty minutes. Early sun (sunrise to ten A.M.) is good to use if you or your partner are tired all the time and have no sexual energy. Late afternoon sun (five P.M. to sunset) is best for healing love or sexual problems; it is the most gentle sun. The midday sun (noon to four P.M.) can be used in small doses (one to three minutes) to create a strong sexual magnetism. Any exposure over three minutes can be harmful or lead to obsessive behavior. As you eat the fruit, imagine your body being filled with the warm, stirring energy of the sun gods Ra, Apollo, and Mithra. These three sun gods are summoned to renew sexual energy.

Feel their strength filling your whole body. If you are feeding the fruit to a partner, take him or her through this visualization. If you are not able to openly communicate what you are doing, then imagine his or her body warming up to the sun and to you. It is best to charge your fruit with solar energy on a Sunday.

UNDER THE TONGUE SPELL

Ingredients:

**cinnamon
cardamom
vanilla bean
chocolate-covered espresso bean**

Certain spices when held under the tongue can promote lustfulness. They can produce lust in another when that person is kissed by you as you hold the spices under your tongue.

Use cinnamon if you want to speed up the events leading to a sexual encounter. Cardamom is used to stimulate your own sex drive. It can also produce feelings of wanton lust in another. Vanilla bean or vanilla extract increases the sexual appetite. Chocolate-covered espresso beans can help increase stamina for lovemaking.

LUST BULB

Ingredients:

**toasted sesame oil
one whole garlic bulb**

tomato or basil leaf
tinfoil

Anoint the garlic by pouring a teaspoon of toasted sesame oil into the palm of your hand. Imagine the object of your desire resting in the palm of your hand as you do so. Give the garlic a long and vigorous rubbing. Then wrap in tinfoil (an attractant) and put in the broiler to roast for thirty-five to forty minutes. Roasting brings the juices of a meat to the surface quickly. Imagine the blood and juices of the desired one heating up for you. When the garlic is done, remove and let cool for just a few minutes until it is cool enough to touch. You want the garlic to remain somewhat hot. Now remove a clove and begin to squeeze the garlic out to form the initials of your desired. Squeeze them out onto a slice of tomato (to attract a woman) or a leaf of basil (to attract a man) and devour them. Call out his/her name and visualize that person's personage as the garlic dissolves in your mouth.

You can also feed your own initials to your intended. However, it is lucky and wise to smear your own initials onto the tomato or basil leaf before feeding it to the desired party. First, it protects you from being too obvious about your feelings, and second, this way the magic will enter through the person's subconscious.

Note: This spell does not result in love. It should be used only for creating sexual attraction between yourself and another party.

RED HOT LOVE STALK SPELL

Ingredients:

strawberry/rhubarb jam

Strawberry/rhubarb jam can literally be used in fertility rites but can also be consumed to give a sexual rebirth to a relationship. Eaten once a month, it can continually fuel the pilot light of love. If your pilot light has gone out, eat some every morning from the new to full moon to reignite the spark in a relationship.

Strawberries are sacred to the love goddess Erzulie. In the voodoo tradition, Erzulie has many aspects. Strawberries invoke her passion and sense of renewal. Rhubarb is sacred to Shangó. In Santeria, he is the god of the drums, the heartbeat, sensuality, and sexuality. Spread this jam on fingers or muffins and consume to fan the flames of desire.

MAENAD SPELL

Ingredients:

black, purple, or red grape clusters

My friend Sylvia drives men mad. Her secret? Syl eats black, purple, and red grape clusters every morning for breakfast. Grapes are sacred to Dionysus, the god of wine, and his priestesses, the maenads. The maenads were infamous for going ''wilding'' in the ancient hills of Greece. They would drink themselves into frenzies, have their way with any man they came across, and then tear him to shreds and devour him.

Sylvia is insatiable. Goddess help any man who crosses her path. She has her way with him, chews him up, and then spits him out. She goes through men like watered wine (or grapes on a vine). These poor fellows usually wind up at my shop looking for the cure to a broken heart.

Grapes (or wine) can be used to release female ferocity. Do not use green grapes (they are for money) unless you are a member of the world's oldest profession. Sylvia says to eat black for power, purple for pleasure, and red for blood. That's what she's out for: to pierce the *corazón,* that muscular organ from which all blood pulses forth. That and that alone satisfies Ms. Syl.

"Yes, I want her powers," you cry. "But what if I want to possess the heart of only one man?" you ask.

Simple, darlings. Just eat one grape, not a cluster. First thing every morning.

RIDING THE BROOMSTICK SPELL

Ingredients:

a broom

According to the Jewish apocryphal writings, Adam had a wife before Eve. Her name was Lilith, and she was banished from the Garden of Eden because she refused to lie in the supine position. God then created the more docile Eve. This spell will align you with the goddess Lilith, the archetype of uncensored expression of female sexuality. Lilith was completely demonized by the rabbinical scholars of the early centuries. Her story was actually removed from the Bible. There are only two fleeting and obscure references to Lilith in the Bible. After her banishment she is said to have led a life of debauchery coupling with demons. Some writings claim she became the concubine of God.

Lilith allows women the freedom to express their sexual needs and desires. She empowers and delights both men and women who are open and enlightened enough to accept her teachings. Lilith heals the sexual hang-ups of the world. She is wise and forgiving and liberating. Nothing scares this queen of the night. Are you feeling vexed about your strict religious upbringing? Don't feel sexy anymore after giving birth? Finding it hard to come to terms with an abortion? Sexual abuse in your childhood? Are these issues ruining your sex life? Ritual can help release the pain and free you to explore your sexuality in safety.

In the Middle Ages the church fathers used the image of a witch riding a broomstick to describe a woman who liked to "ride" on top of a man. This was considered devil's play. Riding the broom is also a euphemism for tantric sex. A broomstick anointed with flying oil was a reference to a dildo used in female masturbation. A woman deriving pleasure without the help of a man was considered so threatening, it was deemed evil. Although we live in the modern age, much of this philosophy has crept its way back in. Straddle forth if you wish to release yourself from the insidious laws of the sex police.

The broomstick spell is for women only. It is performed to increase your own sexual pleasure. It will free your tantric spirit to help you attain pleasure with yourself or with the assistance of a partner. You can do this spell to invoke a better sexual partner, to change the energy between you and your existing partner, or just to help yourself explore your own depths of desire. On a full moon, you will straddle the broom and make a wish. It's as simple as that. Put on your favorite music or music that makes you feel sexually open, and dance with the broom. I encourage you to perform this spell in front of a partner, as it can only help to tune in the partner to your needs. You must work up a sweat dancing with the broom and at the same time work your wish up in your mind to a frenzy. Finally, release the energy, bow to the broom, and thank it.

If you want, you can also jump the broom (with or without your partner). Just be aware that jumping the broom is considered fertility magic. If your partner is capable of getting you pregnant, you will want to think twice before jumping the broom. If you end by jumping the broom, that is a good way to seal off the energy once you have raised it. Imagine the energy flowing out of your feet and into the earth as you land. If you choose not to jump the broom, then bow or curtsy to the broom after you dance and place your hands on the floor to release and ground the energy you have raised. Just let the energy flow from your fingertips into the earth.

It is always important to release energy once you raise it (unless you are purposely storing it for later release). Otherwise the magic will not have a chance to go out into the universe and then come back to you. Think of your energy as a balloon that you are filling with helium. Once the balloon is filled and tied, you must release it and let it float up to the sky goddess. When the sky goddess receives it she will smile down at you and grant you your wish. Lilith, by the way, is associated with the night sky, so it is best to do this ritual at night. The witching hour, to be exact!

SEXUAL PERFORMANCE SPELL

When you boil it all down what does a man really need?
Just a smoke and cup of coffee.

—*Johnny Guitar*

Ingredients:

  coffee
  cigarettes (or a cigar or chewing tobacco)

Certainly not approved by the Food and Drug Administration, these two ingredients, on the surface, seem antithetical to sexuality and physical vigor. Studies may have shown that quitting smoking enhances the sex drive, but personal experience and testimony from friends prove the opposite. Those who survive giving up tobacco usually turn to Prozac for the depression and *voilà!* end of sex drive. Tobacco (in small doses) *is* a sexual stimulant. Just think of all those glamorous gals and guys puffing away in old Hollywood movies. You should, however, use pure, chemically untreated tobacco. Most cigarette manufacturers coat the cigarette paper with saltpeter to keep the stick burning smoothly. Saltpeter (once fed to men in prison) is known to kill the sex drive.

Tobacco and coffee are ruled by Mars, fiery god of war and eternal erections. Cigars are loved by Ellegua, the remover of obstacles, and by that playboy of the Yoruban pantheon, Chango. Tobacco is used in Native American rites for magical purposes, and according to Yuchi* legend, tobacco was born out of semen drops. Sexy, huh?

Although tobacco is traditionally enjoyed after sex, I suggest lighting up before lovemaking, especially if you would like to be able to last for hours. Coffee increases work or performance, and tobacco increases drive. To increase your capacity for pleasure, eat a chocolate-covered cherry with your coffee and smoke. If you are averse to smoking tobacco or drinking coffee, you can take a pinch of tobacco and a teaspoon of fresh coffee grinds (French vanilla and chocolate almond coffee are particularly effective) and rub them together in your palms. Once you have created heat in your hands, brush the coffee and tobacco off your palms and then vigorously rub your whole body down with a quick movement of your hands. This will create more vibrancy in your physical body. If you have allergies or sensitive skin, I do not recommend this method. Instead place a small pouch with coffee and tobacco on your bedroom altar or under the mattress as a talisman to increase sexual performance.

INCUBUS AND SUCCUBUS SPELL

The incubus (male) and succubus (female) are legendary night demons who engage in lascivious sexual activity with men and women, usually during sleep. According to the Talmud, the succubus is responsible for nocturnal emissions. Traditionally seen as harmful, energy-stealing demons, these fallen angels can be warded off by numerous methods. One popular formula to keep incubi and succubi at bay was based on the medieval belief in the power of family values. The names of Adam and Eve, followed by the names of the patriarchs and matriarchs, were written on parchment. Historical documents also include passages of Scripture to ward off Lilith (queen of

*Native American tribe originating in Georgia.

the succubi) and her legions. Lilith was the first wife of Adam. Sources say that after leaving him, she ran off to the desert to couple with demons.

In this day and age of STDs, astral sex may be the only true form of safe sex left to us. What follows are two spells. The first is for traditionalists, to ward off the harmful draining effects of sexual night demons or night*mares*.* The second, for the more daring modern-age crowd, actually invokes a sexual night demon of your very own to end those lonely nights.

To Ward Off

Ingredients:

felt pen
a bowl
spring water
lemon juice
sea salt
red string or ribbon

In ancient Babylonia it was believed one could trap the energies of the incubus or succubus inside an inverted bowl with prayers written on it. There is also a custom of tying a red string or ribbon on the wrist while sleeping or tying it onto the bedpost. Spring water with lemon juice and sea salt is a medieval formula used for dispelling nightmares. Take a wooden bowl and write these words with a felt pen inside the center of the bowl:

> *The Lord bless thee, and keep thee:*
> *The Lord make His face to shine upon thee,*

Mare means ''incubus'' in Old English.

and be gracious unto thee;
the Lord lift up His countenance unto thee; and give thee peace. *

Rub a teaspoon of coarse sea salt, three drops of spring water, and nine drops of lemon juice into its center. Turn the bowl upside-down and place it on your nightstand or underneath the bed. Tie a red ribbon around your wrist. Tie another red ribbon onto the bedpost or frame. Attach a small piece of paper to that ribbon with the words ''Do Not Disturb'' written on it. Sleep tight, and don't let the incubus and succubus bite!

To Attract

Ingredients:

> **red wine (or purple grape juice)**
> **lime juice**
> **walnut shells**
> **goosedown pillow**
> **piece of black leather or black lace or black satin**
> **almond oil**
> **black and red licorice sticks**

Cabalistic legend says that Lilith was born out of the *k'lifot*, the shells. *K'lifot* can refer to any shell or covering, as in the skull that covers the brain or a shell that covers a nut or an egg. The foreskin is considered a form of *k'lifot*. So is afterbirth or the placenta. In matriarchal cultures these coverings were honored for the shelter and nurturing they once provided. In patriarchal societies the chaff becomes not only

---

*Numbers 6:24–26. Traditional verse used to ward off incubus and succubus. Psalm 121 is also used.

useless but evil once separated from the grain. The Hebrew word for shell, skin, or bark is *k'lifah*. The same word also means a female demon. *K'lifat hashum* means a garlic skin or a worthless thing. Shells are considered feminine, useless, and sinful. When Lilith separated from Adam, she became "evil."

Use a walnut shell to attract the tantric lovers of the night. If you want to attract the male of the species, place a small strip of banana peel inside the shell. The incubi and succubi are also attracted to blood. You can use purple grape juice or red wine as a substitute. Place five drops of red wine into the shell. Squeeze five drops of lime juice into the shell for power and influence. Lay the walnut shell on top of a piece of leather or leather garment if you want the sex to be rough. Lay it on lace or silk if you want the sex to be gentle and tender. Make sure the walnut shell is sitting as an open bowl, or you will trap the incubus or succubus when they arrive. Meditate on the little shell bowl and open your mind to the experience. Place your pinkies into the shell and then dab the outer corners of your eyelids. Rub your left big toe with almond oil. It is said that these sexy devils often enter the body through the big toe. Almond oil will attract them and help you to open up your sexual and psychic centers.

Scriptures warn against sleeping naked because it attracts incubi and succubi. **Sleep naked.** Close your eyes and lay your head on a pillow of goosedown. Lilith and her consorts love all feathered things, and goosedown assists with communication on the astral. Begin to think sexy thoughts as you chew on a piece of black or red licorice. Red is for sex. Black is for naughtiness. Licorice stimulates the yin centers and makes us open and receptive to sexual gratification. Count to 666 (the number of the beast) and drift off to sleep. Your dream lover will not enter until you are sound asleep. Of course, some people do not remember their dreams. It would be a shame to forget this strictly taboo encounter after you've gone to all this trouble. Here is a spell to remember your dreams so that you can recall what transpired in the night and then brag to all your friends the next day. (Sex demons don't mind if you kiss and tell.) Before you lay your head on the pillow, drink half a glass of water. The moment you wake up, drink the other half to remember your sweet and sexy dream.

LOVE AND GLAMOUR

Love is not a thing you can possess. Love is not a thing you can make someone do. To enchant, bewitch, throw glamour, witchery, or illusion on another is a different spiritual vibration from the vibration that the natural state of love produces. Of course, glamour is often more predictable and has a better control factor than love.

FISH HEAVEN

Ingredients:

flat fillets of anchovies in pure olive oil, salt added

According to an old Greek legend, anchovies are believed to attract beautiful women. It is said that the anchovies live in the hair of mermaids. From this they glean the magical powers to attract beauty. If you would like to have many beautiful women in your midst, I recommend eating a tin of flat fillets of anchovies in pure olive oil with salt added. You must eat them on a full moon in Pisces, for this is when the spell is most effective. The full moon in Pisces falls once a year when the sun is in the sign of Virgo. (Look for the full moon in late August to mid-September. Check your calendar this year for the exact date.) The second best time is a new moon in Pisces. This is most favorable for meeting new and exciting beautiful women. The new moon in Pisces will happen when the sun is in Pisces. (Look for the new moon in late February to mid-March. Check this year's calendar for the exact date.) The third best time to perform this spell is on a waxing moon in Pisces. For this you will have to pay close attention to your astrological calendar, as there are many waxing moons throughout the year. It is not advisable to perform this spell during a waning moon in Pisces, for you will most assuredly meet a beautiful woman with whom you shall fall in love, and she will then disappear (like the vaporous moon).

THE LONG AND WINDING ROAD (LEADING TO NOWHERE) SPELL

When she said she wanted a long courtship,
I had no idea that meant winter in Siberia.

—*Vladymir Alexandroff*

Ingredients:

> rosebuds
> juniper berries (or a shot of gin)
> cinnamon powder
> three teardrops

Rose, juniper, and cinnamon are traditionally used for fast luck spells. If put on green candles, they bring money fast. If put on red candles, they bring quick results in love. This spell was requested by a certain gentleman friend of mine named Vlad. He had spent an inordinate amount of time and money cultivating a relationship with a certain Russian countess. However, the more money and the more time Vlad spent, the chillier the countess became. It took him seven dates and $7,000 to gain one kiss (a cheeky one, as in delivered to the side of the face). According to my source on the etiquette of dating, three is the magical number upon which one can expect to score. Anyway, Vlad developed a nasty cold from the frosty reproaches of the countess. He came to me down and out and sneezing. Poor man. We crushed some rosebuds together, rubbed them between our fingers, and let the petals fall into a lovely red bowl. I went to look for some juniper berries in my apothecary and discovered I was all out. Vlad, in the meantime, had raided my mad money bowl and gone to the liquor store on the corner. He returned with a bottle of gin and a bottle of tonic.

"How psychic you are, Vladimir!" I exclaimed, and seized the bottle of gin from his hands.

You see, gin is made from juniper berries; therefore it can serve as the modern equivalent of this somewhat hard to obtain herb. I poured a shot of gin into the bowl of rosebuds and swirled it around while Vladimir made us drinks.

"Juniper is ruled by Jove, our benevolent and wise Father. We will ask him for guidance and wisdom on your behalf. Of all the gods, Jove has by far had the most experience with women. He will know how to get to your countess."

"Will he turn me into a swan?" asked Vlad. "Then I could fly into her window and permeate her with my enormous wingspan."

"You wish, darling. Now sshh and let me think," I implored him.

I rummaged through my spice rack to see what else could be found. My intuition told me we needed one or two more ingredients. I stopped to sip my gin and tonic and ponder. If nothing else, I knew that juniper and rose were also used for curing head colds. I could hear Vlad reciting poetry in the other room. Yeats, I think.

> *How can those terrified vague fingers push*
> *The feathered glory from her loosening thighs?*

"Very good invocation, dear. Keep it up," I yelled encouragingly. "You know, the rosebuds are sacred to Venus. We can always use her help in matters such as these."

> *A shudder in the loins engenders there*

The broken wall, the burning roof and tower
And Agamemnon—

"Oh, goddess, I can't go on. Another minute and I shall die," cried Vlad, sobbing.

"Let's try a dash of cinnamon—no, a drizzle. Hmmm, a heaping spoonful would make it sizzle!" I said, running into the living room with the bowl. "Vlad, I'm adding cinnamon to speed things up. Oh, Vlad, you're crying. Well, cry into the bowl if you must. Tears are always good for spells. What god or goddess can resist a man's tears? Come on, darling. Cry away," I said, holding the bowl under Vladimir's eyes. Three huge teardrops plopped into the bowl. A roaring crack of thunder was heard from outside.

"By Jove, I think we've got it," I said with delight, and then I instructed Vlad to mix all the ingredients with his deft digits. He then dusted his whole body down with his hands. He began by rubbing his head and quickly worked his way toward the feet. In most cases anointing should begin in the middle, work upward, back to the middle, and then downward. In Vlad's case, we wanted to bring an idea long loitering in his mind straight down to the feet, or earth plane, which represents physical manifestation.

"Repeat after me," I said, and he did.

"Countess, Countess, come to me by the power of Jove and the number three." I had him chant this three times.

"So mote it be," we recited, and then laughed in unison.

Suddenly Vlad's face turned serious and he said, "I feel a strange vibration in my pants. Are you sure we haven't just performed the succubus spell?"

"I'm quite sure," I said, annoyed at him for thinking me an Aunt Clara. "I'm not a witch to misplace a potion," I added coolly.

Vlad sneezed, and upon a quick pat-down of his pants, he discovered that this strange tingling was coming from his beeper, which he had mistakenly set on pulse. He removed it from his pocket to find the countess's phone number flashing in red. A huge smile and the flashing of wolves' teeth appeared as he dialed her number. I mixed him a drink for the road and eavesdropped on the call. It seemed the countess was very taken by the seven dozen long-stemmed roses that had just arrived, and she wanted him to arrive as well. Pronto! He hung up the phone happy as could be, downed his drink, and asked me if he could borrow cabfare. (Apparently he had dropped his last dollar at the florist's earlier that evening.)

I understand he spent the next seven nights in sexual bliss with the countess. Finally their long courtship has ended. Yesterday the countess rang me up to ask for a marriage spell. I just hope Vlad doesn't ask to borrow cash for the ring!

BEWITCHING MIRROR SPELL

Ingredients:

> **a mirror**
> **three drops of apple cider vinegar**
> **ammonia or glass cleaner**
> **white magnolia soap**

We all know there are wicked mirrors and wonderful mirrors. Wicked mirrors make us look fat and ugly. Wonderful mirrors make us look thin and beautiful. I have seen many a vexed mirror in my day. Here is how to uncross a vexed mirror. Add three drops of apple cider vinegar to a spray bottle filled with a capful of ammonia and ten ounces of spring water. You may also use a traditional glass cleaner (as long as it contains ammonia) and add three drops of apple cider vinegar to that. Cover the entire mirror with a light mist and then wipe clean in counterclockwise circles. Repeat this chant three times: "I banish all that's wicked in the glass. Do not another evil image cast."

Then, moving in a clockwise direction, mark the four corners of your mirror with the white magnolia soap. Begin in the upper left-hand corner and work your way round. Make sure that you return to the upper left-hand corner so that you have made a complete circle around the mirror. Just brush the soap across the glass enough to leave a small mark. As you do this, chant three times: "Mirror mirror on the wall, who's the fairest of them all? Me! Me! Me!"

Ammonia drives away evil and envious spirits. Spirits are known to hide in mirrors, and sometimes they are envious of the living, so they create nasty illusions to scare the living or to make the living despise themselves (or at least contribute to their low self-esteem). Apple cider vinegar will attract loving, doting spirits who will delight in showing you how beautiful you are, inside and out. Magnolia is a flower of dreams and glamour. Magnolia will help your mirror create stunning supermodel illusions, thereby boosting your confidence to mammoth proportions. Remember, you're only as pretty as you feel, and good lighting is everything!

ENCHANTED MIRROR SPELL

Ingredients:

> **a large mirror and a small mirror**
> **three drops of apple cider vinegar**
> **ammonia or glass cleaner**
> **white magnolia soap**
> **small piece of ivory-colored silk or nylon stocking**
> **strand of cornsilk**

Ever have one of those days when you leave home looking just so? The household mirror affirms that you are looking good. Then you pass some nasty reflective glass in the big bad world, stop to gaze, say, "Oh, my God," and every bone in your body makes you want to turn and run for home. Even if you overcome this compulsion and keep going along your way, you wonder all day, What do I really look like?

Now, it is impossible to fix all the demon street or mall mirrors in your town, but this spell will show you how to create a warrior talisman against boogyglass. This charm can also make sure that others see you the same way you see yourself in your own spellbound mirror. You will need a small mirror or piece of mirror (something small enough to carry in a pocket). Do not break a mirror to obtain this ingredient, and do not choose anything with sharp or jagged edges. Best choice is removing a small mirror from an old compact or lipstick case. Perform the Bewitching Mirror Spell on the small mirror. Before you leave your house, admire your image in the large mirror. Then hold the little mirror up to the large mirror so that the reflective sides are facing each other. Say *"Backatcha backatcha backatcha,"** and then wrap the little mirror in a piece of ivory- or nude-colored silk. You may use a piece of nylon stocking in a pinch; however, if you do so, you must first wrap one strand of cornsilk around the mirror. The silk has the practical purpose of protecting the glass and the magical purpose of preserving the life of the magic you have raised. Carry this talisman in your front coat pocket, breast pocket, or bra with the reflective side out. You will never have to double-check your image again.

BOHEMIAN LOVE SPELL

Si tu ne m'aimes pas, je t'aime;
Si je t'aime, prends garde à toi**

—*Carmen*

Ingredients:

  assorted flowers

*Modern mystical incantation. Translation: Back at you.
**If you don't love me, I love you;
  If I love you, watch out!

What do William Shakespeare and Georges Bizet have in common? Both neglected to name the flower. In *A Midsummer Night's Dream,* Oberon, the Fairy King, has Puck, a fairy, fetch him a certain flower to cast a love spell.

> *Yet mark'd I where the bolt of Cupid fell:*
> *It fell upon a little western flower,*
> *Before milk-white, now purple with love's wound . . .*

It is rumored that in the garden of Eden, Eve kissed a white rose. The rose blushed out of desire and has remained pink to this very day. In Greek lore the rose is said to have been created by the gods to celebrate the birth of Aphrodite. One myth says the rose turned red because Aphrodite pricked her feet and drew blood on the thorns while she was looking for Adonis. Another legend says her son Cupid spilled wine on it by accident, turning it a purplish red. Yet another legend claims Cupid stopped to smell the rose and was stung by a bee. He became angry and shot an arrow into the bush. The arrows became the thorns. In any case, it becomes clear that the rose can prick not only the finger, but also the heart.

Oberon tells Puck that the juice of this flower placed on the sleeping eyelids of either a man or a woman will cause that person to fall madly in love with the first *live creature* he or she sees upon awakening. If you feel your husband/wife, boyfriend/ girlfriend, is falling out of love with you, place some moist red or purple rose petals on his/her sleeping eyelids. Just make sure he or she sees you—and not the dog— upon first awakening.

One of the most popular surnames of Gypsies is Faa or Fay or Fairy. The Gypsies, or Romanies, worshiped the Earth Mother and were said to know the magic of the fairy folk. In *Carmen,* the opera by Georges Bizet, the Gypsy Carmen casts a love spell on the soldier Don José. She does this by taking an enchanted flower from her corset and throwing it at José. He then falls desperately in love with her, against his better judgment. The words "corsage" and "corset" have the same root: *cors,* which means "body" in Old French. To take a corsage from your corset and toss it at another will make them desire your body. It will also put them completely into their own bodies, allowing lust to take over and removing any form of mental resistance.

Another form of this ritual continues to thrive in modern day. Custom still dictates that a gentleman deliver an orchid to his date on prom night. He will traditionally pin the corsage to her hand, bosom, or bodice. The word "orchid" comes from a Greek word meaning "testicle." So the gentleman is symbolically implanting his seed, the hopes of his future offspring, into the heart and body of the woman. (I bet that will give you second thoughts about letting your daughter go to the prom.) If it's the hand, he is asking for her hand in marriage. In occult workings the orchid is prized for its magical power of concentration. If the magician can focus upon his will, he will be able to evoke physical manifestation. He will be able to create life. It is one of the most exotic and erotic magical flowers. Do not use orchids unless you mean to play for keeps—and for future generations.

By contrast, if a woman throws a flower (orchid or otherwise) that has been lodged in her bosom or corset at a man, it does not mean she wants to bear his children. It simply means she is offering him something he will not be able to resist. If, however, she were to pin the flower to his pants fly, I suppose they would end up making babies. (Personally, I have never seen this done.)

If one person holds a red rose between their teeth, and another person takes that rose from them using their own teeth, those two people will have sex before the night is through. If said parties are dancing to Gypsy or flamenco music while they make this transaction, the sex will be wonderfully fulfilling for both parties.

A white rose given means you want to maintain a platonic relationship with someone. Yellow roses connote jealousy and are not favored for casting love spells unless you want to make someone jealous and possessive over you. A pink rose is for flirtation and sexuality. A red rose with thorns is used to prick someone's heart. Similar to the orchid, it implies you would like to entrust not only yourself but your progeny to this person's heart. The fleur-de-lis is a very magical flower with a long history. Some say the fleur-de-lis is an iris. In French it translates to "flower of lily." The fleur-de-lis is also known as a frog, a sewing term denoting a clasp with three woven rings. This fleur-de-lis is sacred to Hecate, queen of the witches. To run any flower stem through the three rings of the fleur-de-lis is a way to empower that flower. Finally, brush the flower against your lips before throwing it at another person. If they catch it, they will be rendered powerless under your spell. If it lands at their feet, they'd better watch out, as they will surely trip and fall madly in love with you.

A flower you have brushed against your genitals, breasts, and lips can strongly affect an unsuspecting partner. Right breast to left breast to genitals and back to right breast forms the sacred triangle. This will create lust or promote fertility in a relationship. To create a purely romantic attraction, brush the flower from the right breast to the left breast to the lips and back to the right breast. Do both brushings if you want to create an upper and lower triad of love—romantic and sexual.

Dancing around a flower, working up a sweat, and anointing the fragrant flower with a drop of your own sweat is very magical, especially if the flower is extremely fragrant, like the gardenia, for example. After orchids, gardenias hold the most power in love. Next is jasmine, then rose. Many supermarkets or open markets sell fresh flowers. They are quite easy to obtain. Pressing flowers is another way to create a magic spell. Take a diary and write down all the things you wish for yourself in love or all the things you wish for yourself and another specific person you are in love with. Now press a fragrant flower into that page and leave the book closed for an entire new-to-full-moon cycle. On the full moon open the book and let the fragrance embrace your nostrils. In the same way your sweet wishes will embrace your life.

If you pick a flower that a bee or a butterfly has recently passed over, that flower will have the power to enchant another. It is said that the union resulting from this particular magic will last until death do you part.

DREAM LOVER SPELL

Ingredients:

mushrooms

Mushrooms are the *nudgers and shovers* of the magical world. They inhabit the be-witching woods and are sacred to fairies and wood nymphs. According to my friend Connie, wood mushrooms taste entirely different from supermarket mushrooms. You can taste and smell the woods in them. Connie speaks of the queen of mushrooms, known as the *Mama Funge*. Three times the size of a cauliflower, the *Mama Funge* is the most powerful edible mushroom in existence. If eaten, she can grant wishes and cast illusions to make anyone fall in love with you. Connie says if you are going to pick wild mushrooms, obtain a good guide book and pay attention to the birds. If a bird picks on a wild mushroom, you know it will probably be edible.

Who hasn't heard of the *magic mushroom* known for its great hallucinogenic pow-ers? Mushrooms literally can make us trip. Some mushrooms are hallucinogenic, some poisonous, some edible and wonderful. All mushrooms are magical. Mushrooms are also ruled by the moon and Neptune. The moon is the most amorous orb and can create more or less of a situation depending on whether you do your spell during a waxing or a waning moon. Master of drugs, fantasy, and the imagination, Neptune can be dreamy and utopian. He can also be false and create deception. If you are fantasizing too much, stay away from mushrooms. However, if your life has become too mundane, you need an infusion of mushrooms.

I have found mushrooms to be quite effective for clients who have mad crushes from afar yet find it difficult to get up close to the object of their desire. To creep into someone's life and eventually take over, just remember the basic law of mush-room magic: Numbers rule. Once you begin a mushroom spell you must maintain it constantly or the illusion will break. Traditionally, a witch would go into the woods and plant her wish underneath a mushroom. As the mushrooms began to sprout all around, so her wish would sprout and grow. The witch could rely on the power of nature to sustain the wish, as mushrooms can be trusted to continually reproduce in the woods. You will have to repeat this spell every new moon until you are quite sure you have your foot planted firmly in the door. The new-to-full-moon period is approximately fourteen to sixteen days. On a new moon you will eat one mushroom, the next day you will eat two mushrooms, the third day you will eat three mushrooms, and so on, until the day of the full moon, when you will eat anywhere from fourteen to sixteen mushrooms. Each day you will visualize yourself getting closer and closer to the person (or situation) you desire. Hold the mushroom(s) in your hands while you do this visualization. Cup your hands over the mushrooms when you have the image clearly in your mind. Then eat the mushrooms while still holding these thoughts. You must not be interrupted during this ritual. Choose a time during the day or evening when you know you will not be disturbed.

Mushroom soup will create more romance in the life. Eat alone or with a partner on a full moon. Mushroom gravy can be served to a mate to open him/her up to taking a dream or fantasy vacation.

Have you ever had the experience of traveling in dreamland together with your lover? Poppy seeds and dried mushrooms will make a person dream about you or you dream about him/her. Place under both pillows to dream about each other.

Tea made with dried mushrooms can be served to someone over whom you want to cast illusions. The larger the mushroom, the larger the illusion you can create. If you like to tell tall tales to get girls, it is best to carry a dried mushroom in your pocket. That way your illusions will be believed and you will never be found out.

BATHING BEAUTIES AND SHOWER POWER

A word about the difference between magical bathing and showering. Bathing is yin, receptive. Showering is yang, aggressive. Bathe when you want to open up and pull someone into your aura. Shower when you want to push your way into someone else's force field or circle of energy.

Most recipes are given in bath form. If you do not have a bathtub (a common phenomenon in New York City, although probably unheard of in the rest of the United States), simply convert the spell for a shower. The procedure with showers is as follows: Take a shower as usual, shampoo hair, soap down, and so on. After you are physically clean, pour over your head a bucket of warm water filled with all magical ingredients required for the spell. Do not rinse off again after this procedure. Towel or air dry. If a spell requires you to rub something sticky into the body (such as in the Honey Three Spell), you can do this standing in the shower, and you may rinse off afterward (with water only).

LOVE HEALING BATH

Ingredients:

    carnations, white or pink
    bubble bath with rosemary or aloe

This bath is best utilized by couples and performed on a regular basis. Bickering is a common pastime, and this ritual can help remove the negative residue that tends to build up between couples. It is great for removing and healing little resentments that tend to accumulate over time. Try taking the bath with your partner or taking turns giving the bath to each other.

This bath is also good for an individual who has been deeply hurt in a relationship. You cannot truly move on until you have healed your heart. In this case it is best to give yourself the bath unless you can find a priestess to assist.

Carnations are used in the Caribbean to cleanse sickness from the body or heart. Usually the voodoo or Wiccan priestess will lightly beat the subject with fresh carnations to remove any negative emotions or illness from the heart and/or body. If you can do this for another or have someone do it to you, that would be ideal. Otherwise you may do it for yourself. The most important thing is to break the stems of the carnations after you have cleansed yourself. If you are feeling particularly distressed, begin by taking three to five white carnations and brushing yourself lightly from head to toe with the flowers. Make sure the stems are long enough so you can reach behind you as if you were using a back scratcher to reach those hard-to-get places. Use strong pressure behind the shoulder blades, as this is a spot where the body tends to store hidden pain (behind the neck as well). When you reach the feet be sure to pull the flowers between each toe. Do not worry if some petals come loose as you do this. When you are done, break the stems in half. This is a very important part of the ritual. The flowers have just absorbed the sickness, anger, pain, or sorrow that lay within you. By breaking the stems, you insure that energy remains trapped in the carnation to die along with the flower. Many ancient cultures believed in sacrificing animals or plants to take away human pain or sin. These practices continue today within Santeria and Judaism. In Santeria chickens or plants are used to cleanse humans. Before Yom Kippur Jewish people use roosters and hens to remove sin (although it is permitted to substitute by giving money to charity). In the ancient pagan cultures the king was sacrificed once a year to protect the entire tribe and all their crops. Today witches substitute a wicker man (doll fashioned out of straw) and burn him at the autumn equinox.

After you have broken the stems on the white carnations, prepare a bath with aloe, rosemary, and fresh pink carnations. The rosemary is to remind you of the positive healing effects of loving and opening your heart. The aloe is used to strengthen and heal the emotional centers that have been weakened. The pink carnations are to cleanse the physical or sexual centers. (The white were used to cleanse the heart and mind as well as the spiritual centers.) If there have been ugly words, use red carnations as well. Insert one and hold it in the mouth for twenty to thirty seconds. Then remove and rub vigorously up and down the throat chakra before breaking its stem. Rub the pink carnations over the whole body while in the bath. After all the water has drained, stand up, break the stems, and step out of the bathtub. Wrap yourself in a white or pink towel and allow yourself to air dry. If this bath is being done as a couple, lie down together for at least forty minutes. Whisper and caress each other. You may make love, but allow yourselves the forty cooing minutes before you engage in any sexual activity. If you are alone, follow up the bath by mirror gazing for at least twenty minutes. Look at yourself in the mirror and whisper beautiful and affirming things to yourself. Do not skip this part of the ritual. Even if it makes you feel silly, it is just as important as the bath.

VENUS SCRUB

Ingredients:

   copper scourer

Copper is sacred to Venus. The skin is ruled by Libra, and Venus is the planetary ruler of Libra. The skin is the largest organ of the body and one of the most seductive.

In ancient as well as modern times, women and men have applied numerous scrubs to the skin to enhance their sexuality. One of the oldest methods of pampering the skin is the dry scrub, also known as body brushing. It removes dead cells from the epidermis, increases circulation, and invigorates the skin.

Take a copper scourer and brush the skin. You will have to judge your own body to see how gentle or hard you can scrub. I prefer a strong scrub, but those who have sensitive skin must be careful. The body should be dry, and so should the scourer. Always brush toward the heart, never away from the heart. When you brush the stomach, move up the right side and down the left. If you brush the face, breasts, or genital area, be very, very gentle (please). Body brushing is traditionally done with special sauna brushes made out of boar bristle. If you use a copper scourer, you can infuse Venusian vibrations into your skin. The skin and aura will then radiate this energy out and increase your sexual magnetism.

SPELL TO MEND A BROKEN HEART OR TO SOOTHE FEELINGS OF LOVE

Ingredients:

> **rosewater**
> **fresh lilacs**
> **sea salt**

Many supermarkets sell fresh-cut flowers, and these have been used magically in many different cultures. One of the most common uses of flowers in love magic is to decorate an altar (see ''Love Altars'').

It is also traditional to save the flowers, hang them to dry, and use them in your bathwater or added to a potpourri. With this spell there are three ways to approach the magic. First is simply to bathe in the flowers. Fill a tub with warm water, add three fistfuls of salt, a cup of rosewater, and a dozen lilacs. Immerse yourself in the bath for ten minutes. This method is very effective for relieving stress due to what is known or termed as *"lovesickness."* Rub the flowers into the body. Pay special attention to the heart chakra. After you have soaked for ten minutes, rubbing the flowers all over your body and pouring water over your head and back using a glass or shell, then you must break the stems of all the flowers and remove yourself from the tub. Leave all ingredients in the tub until the water has completely drained, then gather up the broken flowers and dispose of them.

The second method is the dry version. Its effects are slightly different from those with the bathing method. But feel free to use it as a complete and effective substitute if you do not have access to a bathtub. This method is a form of dry smudging practiced by Native South and North Americans. The dry method involves beating the body lightly from head to toe with a dozen fresh lilacs. It is best to have a priestess of Wicca or even a good friend do this for you. It is, however, just as effective to perform it on yourself. Just make sure you take the time to reach all the areas (especially on the back) of the body. The difference between the dry and wet method is as follows: The wet method relieves emotional obsessiveness and drains the body of disturbing thoughts and feelings related to the person you are obsessing over. If performed properly, it produces a state of forgetfulness with the side effects of extreme drowsiness. The dry method will not bring the soothing qualities of forgetfulness. It will not make you sleepy, either. The dry method is meant to quickly pull energy off of you so that you can go out in the world and perform in the way that you need to without the obsessive thoughts prompting you to take self-destructive actions.

The third method involves placing lilacs around the home or adding them to a bucket of warm water, sea salt, and rosewater to create the magical floor wash or home bath. Using the floor wash and following up by keeping fresh lilacs in the home is the most effective method and can produce long-term effects. Remember to change the flower water every day to day and a half. This method is most effective for people who are lovesick because a partner has moved from the home. Memories haunt you and cause obsessive thoughts or behavior. The home needs to be cleansed so your healing process can begin and you can move on.

LIVING WELL LADY SPELL

Never argue with a German if you're tired.
—Grace Slick

Ingredients:

   champagne
   caviar
   dark chocolate–covered orange peel

Fräulein Kleinelamm and Herr Ingbone parted ways after a somewhat luxurious life together. The parting was difficult, as Kleinelamm believed it to be a trial separation until Ingbone showed up to pack his bags with his new girlfriend, the affluent divorcée Frau Schwarzes-Loch (also known as Ms. A'Biess). Kleinelamm was beside herself. Now Ingbone was gone for good.

Weeks went by, and the gossip round the *Nachbarschaft* (the 'hood) reported that Herr Ingbone and Ms. A'Biess were experiencing bliss in bed. Kleinelamm wanted to do a spell to squelch any pleasure her Ingbone might be experiencing in the depths of that nasty Schwarzes-Loch. She wanted to do a spell to expose the woman for the no-talent she really was. After many a night of caustic and bitter thoughts, Kleinelamm realized that what she really wanted was a spell to get Herr Ingbone back. Unfortunately, Ms. A'Biess had performed some very powerful void of course moon magic, and now Ingbone, dazzled by her spell, could no more easily find his way back to Kleinelamm than he could find a *Nadel* in a *Heuschober*.*

Realizing that sad reality, Kleinelamm heaved a deep sigh and began to focus on her career. What else was to be done? (Besides, she had to pay her own rent now. Without Herr Ingbone's salary, she could no longer afford to live in the style she had taught Ingbone to become accustomed to.)

Several months passed, and in that time Kleinelamm went underground to develop her great art. She was catering and bartending for a living and painting great master-pieces on the side. Concurrently, Herr Ingbone and Ms. A'Biess were seen smooching at all the important gallery openings. Kleinelamm tried her best to tune out this gossip. Finally it became unbearable. That's when I received a call.

"Please come over. I need to be beaten with carnations and smudged with sage," she pleaded.

Now Kleinelamm is the kind of sweet and beautiful soul that one can never say no to. Besides, I was too tired to argue with her. So I appeared at her modest home with my supplies. I let myself in. Kleinelamm was already running a bath.

"I'm getting in," she shouted through the door.

It was difficult to hear her, as she had Wagner's "Liebestod" blasting on the stereo. (You know, that beautiful and moving, yet unutterably depressing, death song between the lovers Tristan and Isolde? I used to date a German and he loved to come to that music. Personally I found it rather morbid. I mean, death is so inevitable; love and life, so unpredictable and cherishable—why mix the two before they are ordained to meet?) I switched the Wagner for a passionate tango CD.

Taking off my cloak, I noticed a bottle of Veuve Clicquot** and a tin of Beluga caviar on the table. Oh, dear, I thought, I hope she isn't living beyond her means again. I dropped my bag of supplies and entered the bathroom with one aforemen-tioned extravagance held high in each hand.

*Oh, c'mon, *needle* in a *haystack*. You know that!
**Expensive French champagne.

She looked up and with a blushing smile said: "Oh, those! Left-over booty from that Russian countess wedding I catered last night."

I smiled, relieved. Then I noticed the box of Godiva chocolates on the tub ledge.

"Those I paid for," Kleinelamm said with a sigh. "Comfort food. So, where's the sage?" she asked, looking round.

"Darling, here is my wise counsel. I think it's time to try a different approach. Something more extravagant and celebratory," I said, popping the cork on the *Clicquot*. I immediately poured the champagne over her head, sending her into shivers of excited giggles.

"A champagne bath?" questioned Kleinelamm as she threw back her head and opened her mouth.

"Yes," I said, aiming the bubbly directly between her lips. "A champagne-and-caviar bath, that's what you need. I'm channeling this directly from the goddess. You need an extravagant form of healing," I said while anointing her *Lippen* and *Brustwarzen** with caviar.

Her eyes opened adorably wide and she asked: "What does caviar do?"

"What is caviar but fish eggs! Fish are for fertility and wealth. Eggs are for rebirth. In ancient Greece fish and eggs were offered to Hecate, queen of the witches and goddess of the crossroads. She was the revealer of destiny, and the offerings were left to petition her help in choosing the right course in life. You, my darling, are at the crossroads of your life. We will ask Hecate to choose the next road for you to travel. The champagne is for the celebration of your new rich, rewarding, and productive life," I said, making a toast with the bottle.

"But will I find love?" asked Kleinelamm with a darling pout.

"Hmm," I mused, eying the gold-and-red-lace-trimmed box of Godiva chocolates. "Suck on this, darling," I said, inserting my left thumb and a luscious piece of dark chocolate into her mouth.

---

*I think you should figure these out for yourself.

"Mmm, there's an orange inside," she cooed, licking her lips.

"Excellent. Chocolate and oranges. Love in abundance," I said, and then kissed her wet forehead good night.

"Tschüs," she hissed, and kissed me back on the lips.

*"Tschüs,"** I echoed while licking the remnants of salty fish from my lips. I grabbed my cape and bag and let myself out.

In the months that passed, Kleinelamm labored and gave birth to a number of wonderful paintings. She got a show in a very prestigious gallery. A certain Graf** Schatzkammer attended the opening and paid a pretty penny (make that top dollar— no, more like a million marks) for all her works. It was quite impressive. Art aficionados clamored around Kleinelamm, commissioning her for new work; waving checkbooks and large sums of money at her as she and her friends exited the gallery. Amid all this exciting frenzy, they spied Herr Ingbone and Ms. A'Biess having a huge and nasty public argument. Graf Schatzkammer quickly shuffled all members of the party into his limo and headed for the Water Club. He entered with a flourish and ordered champagne and caviar all around to celebrate Kleinelamm's successful debut (and maybe Herr Ingbone's downfall). After many dates Graf invited Kleinelamm to come with him to Buenos Aires. Of course, she accepted, as she needed a holiday after all her hard work. While packing her bags, she received a phone call from Herr Ingbone. He said he wanted her back. He told her that life with Ms. A'Biess was the pits. When could he see her? Herr Ingbone pleaded tearfully.

"As soon as I get home from Buenos Aires," said Kleinelamm calmly. She then slowly hung up the phone and screamed and danced for joy. She composed herself once more to enter the stretch limo that had arrived compliments of Graf Schatzkammer.

She and Graf had a wonderful time in Buenos Aires, where they danced many a

*The parting words, as in "So long," "Cheerio," or "Good night."
**Count.

hot horizontal (as well as vertical) tango. When she returned home, she and Ingbone began to have some long talks.

Postscript: Kleinelamm has informed me that she has given up chocolate. Graf Schatzkammer and Herr Ingbone now provide her with all the love a woman could ever desire. Besides, she wants to keep that beautiful figure.

LOVE TALK

GETTING TO KNOW YOU SPELL

Ingredients:

    crushed walnuts
    nutmeg powder
    cinnamon powder

Historically and cross-culturally, love spells have always included sprinkling herbs or drawing *veves* (magical seals) across thresholds where *l'objet aimé* is destined to walk across. This spell should be performed before said person is to enter your home. The best method is to sprinkle the ingredients under a doormat the person will walk across. You will want to be diligent in sweeping or vacuuming up once the person has crossed over and before another steps across. This is not a spell to perform when a crowd is expected. This is best accomplished when the person you desire will be coming alone to your home or place of work.

    Walnuts have an effect on the brain. They physically resemble the brain, which is why they are magically associated with it. Walnuts and nutmeg combined can create a psychic bond between you and another person. The added cinnamon creates a heat or physical opening as well. This formula is great for overcoming formalities and shyness. It is also works to find where your deep levels of connection are (without taking years to do so). This spell will not create anything that does not exist. Rather, it quickly draws forward the magic and soul connection that already lives between you.

Do not use this spell if you are hiding or concealing something about yourself. The other person will be able to pick up on that. Also do not use if you are spooked by intensity. If you use this spell, the person may very likely walk into your home and walk directly to your most intimate corner within that room. You must be willing to share and be open yourself to work this spell.

You can also dust your hands with this mixture and then touch your temples before entering the home of someone you like. You will find that he or she opens up, revealing many special things to you. You will also find yourself automatically walking toward objects or things in the room that symbolize the deepest connection that exists between you.

I must emphasize that this spell is not necessarily going to bring forth sexual intimacy. (It will if that is the strongest karmic bond between you.) There are numerous spells for that purpose. This spell is to open the mental, emotional, and spiritual life between you. To work the spell, simply crush five walnuts (shelled) in a mortar and pestle. Add a teaspoon of nutmeg and a half teaspoon of cinnamon powder. Sprinkle under the doormat or rug anywhere from forty to thirteen minutes before he or she is scheduled to arrive. Remember to sweep up once the person has left.

SPELL FOR COMMUNICATION IN LOVE

Ingredients:

   clementines
   fresh parsley
   mint (optional)

This is another recipe to promote communication in love. Parsley is the mercurial networker, the telephone operator (Internet server) of spices, if you will. Parsley not only makes good connections, it also appeases bad spirits and drives them away. The custom of placing a sprig of parsley next to cooked-meat dishes stems from an ancient custom based on the belief that the parsley would appease the spirits of the dead animals. The modern carryover remembers only that parsley sweetens and lightens the breath after the heady taste of meat. Use parsley to drive away the ghosts of love.

Oranges are the fruit of love. Clementines are considered to be a bit more energetic than plain old oranges. They also are considered a *talky* fruit. Parsley and orange together will promote communication in love. The parsley can remove ''bad spirits'' such as old baggage that creates fear in association with love and commitment. This is an especially good blend for those whose tongues stumble over the L-word.

If you or your mate are having problems communicating about your sexual needs, add mint to the recipe. Mint brings the element of sexuality and lust to the orange's heart and love vibrations and parsley's communication vibes. You can bathe in orange and parsley (and mint), or open an orange and eat a slice together with a sprig of parsley. You can also rub parsley and orange rind into the skin or simply smell the orange and parsley together to promote communication and openness in love. If the communication problems involve listening to each other, rub the ingredients over the ears so that you will be able to hear one another.

This recipe can also be used to open channels for a new love. In this case, make a tea of parsley, then add a slice of orange and a cinnamon stick to convert to a catch a new love spell.

LOVE'S MESSENGER

Ingredients:

Creamsicle (orange sherbet and vanilla ice cream)

Orange and vanilla can stimulate the sexual appetite and send astral messages of love to someone who is far away. Eat orange sherbet and vanilla ice cream and send thoughts of love to a distant someone. Or take a Creamsicle and write the name of someone you miss on the wooden stick. Let it sit out in a bowl and melt at room temperature. As the Creamsicle melts, this person will melt as well with loving thoughts of you. This spell is effective for those distant in miles as well as those distant in emotion.

CYBERSEX SPELL

Ingredients:

   little red chili peppers
   little red cherry tomatoes
   baby carrots
   fresh dill
   fresh mint

If you are practicing safe sex by having cybersex on-line, this spell is for you. It will help you cut through hours of red tape in the chat rooms and draw that special someone who communicates just the way your heart and head desire. The ingredients are a combination of Mercurial, Martian, and Venusian energies. Mercury stimulates communication and together with Venus helps to send out messages to attract the right partner. The Mars element heats things up sexually, and combined with Mercury, it makes sex talk. Try this formula the next time you go on-line.

Lay out a piece of tinfoil on the table where you keep your computer. Place five red chili peppers, seven red cherry tomatoes, and five baby carrots on the foil. Sprinkle with dill and mint leaves. Fold up the tinfoil and place it on or near your computer.

Now get on-line and search and destroy. I mean search and employ. I mean search and find joy. **:)**

P.S. Do not attempt this spell during a Mercury retrograde. (Check your astrological calendar to find out when these are occurring.)

P.P.S. Is your partner more interested in his/her hard drive than in his/her sex drive? If so, place this foil pouch under your bed. Under the computer table, place a dark and dirty dish towel with nine match heads, a cup of sea salt, and a teaspoon of cayenne pepper wrapped within its folds. This is a get-away formula. It should repel your partner from the computer while the foil pouch attracts your mate into bed.

SPELL FOR TRUST AND UNDERSTANDING

Ingredients:

> **dried red rose petals**
> **whole nutmeg (or powdered)**
> **whole vanilla bean**
> **cinnamon powder**
> **bowl and a wooden spoon**

This spell is modified from a New Orleans voodoo recipe known as Goona Goona powder. You will need some powdered nutmeg, some vanilla powder (take a vanilla bean and grind it up in a coffee grinder to create the powder), three dried red rose petals, and some cinnamon powder. Cinnamon has the property of directness and quickly encourages the opening of lines of communication. Nutmeg promotes vision and truthfulness. Rose and vanilla open up feelings of love and trust. The combination of all four ingredients promote truthfulness, trust, and communication in love. Use this recipe when you need to talk about problems in the relationship or to promote feelings of trust so that you and your partner can open up and speak from the heart.

Make a potpourri with these ingredients and leave out in the open, in a bedroom, family room, or kitchen, to encourage positive communication. Crush a handful of dried rose petals, crack a whole nutmeg with a mortar and pestle or add powdered nutmeg, add powder from a whole vanilla bean, and sprinkle a teaspoon of cinnamon powder into a bowl. Mix all ingredients with a wooden spoon. Wood has the magical properties of channeling the positive and healing forces in nature. The spoon is a nurturing utensil. It scoops up and holds. Also think of spooning: a very nurturing way of sleeping with a loved one. Using a wooden spoon to stir will add emotional strength and support to the potion. You can also dust your hands with these herbs if you are going over to visit your partner or will be meeting in a place where you cannot comfortably leave out a potpourri mixture. A ouanga bag can also be created and carried. Sprinkle the mixture around the telephone before making that call to promote openness and communication. This is also an excellent potpourri to have on the coffee table of your office if you are a couples therapist.

SPELL TO PLEASE YOUR LOVER

Ingredients:

whole raw almonds

Splitting an almond in half inside your mouth (with your teeth) and then rolling your tongue along the smooth center of the nut can help you intuit how to please your lover. Almonds are a food of wealth, but they also rule sensuality, communication, pleasure, and the psychic senses. A tantric nut, if you will, the almond can release a hidden or stored wealth of pleasure. Eat almonds in bed with a lover. This spell is especially useful if there have been sexual problems or dissatisfaction due to miscommunication about lovemaking. It can also be used for couples just getting to know each other or in cases where one or the other is too shy to reveal his/her desires.

SPELL TO ENTER SOMEONE'S DREAMS

Ingredients:

> **whole nutmeg**
> **a crystal (optional)**
> **a small object that has been touched by the dreamer**
> **a goosedown feather from a pillow**
> **a silk scarf**
> **star anise**

This spell begins by making a dream bag or pillow, which you will place underneath or on top of your regular bed pillow. Wrap all ingredients in a silk scarf and tie the scarf in a knot. You can also sew the scarf together to make a pouch or pillow. Nutmeg is a spice endowed with psychic strength. Crystals help to focus and empower our magical energy. A small object touched by the dreamer will create a sympathetic link with the person you are trying to reach (the dreamer). You may use a pen, a scrap of paper, a key, or a matchbook, anything he or she has touched. I emphasize the word *small* only as it will be difficult to fit under your pillow items such as elephants, home entertainment systems, stretch limos, or revolving glass doors to office buildings! A goosedown feather from a pillow will help you fly right inside the dreamer's head. Silk is used to contain and protect magical talismans. Star anise helps one to enter the realm of the astral. Many excellent books have been written on astral travel. The basic rule of thumb is to see yourself rising above your physical body. Just make sure you cord yourself to your physical body so that you can find your way back.

Some people allow their astral bodies to transform into birds for swiftness in flight. Visualize wings sprouting from your astral body (an astral body is similar to your shadow except it is made up of spectral light). See yourself flying to the room in which your friend is sleeping. If you do not know where that is, then simply visualize the top of this person's head. Once you find the object of your desire, lightly beat your wingtips upon the person's brow. Do this six or seven times. At any point in this procedure, if you feel yourself slipping away, rub the pouch you have created to strengthen your power on the astral plane. Imagine your astral body becoming a vapor of light. Let that light or vapor seep into the nostrils, ears, mouth, and corners of the eyes of the dreamer. Once you have visualized this, let the thought go. Focus once again on your dream bag and think of the thoughts you want the dreamer to dream. Although these ingredients do increase power in the astral and dream world, there are those with natural ability for astral travel and those whose ability is not very developed. The success of this spell depends mostly upon the degree of skill of the practitioner. If you are beginning, you will find the pouch very useful. When you become more skilled you may find that the pouch is no longer necessary.

You may also make a request before falling off to sleep to dream about the person you desire or to obtain information about him or her.

SPELL TO ATTRACT THE RIGHT COUPLES THERAPIST

Ingredients:

> **caraway**
> **dill**
> **parsnip**
> **orange and pink candles**

Caraway, dill, and parsnip are herbs of communication as well as herbs of love. Orange candles are used for communication, attraction, and success. Pink candles are used for relaxation, healing the heart, and stimulating positive sexual feelings. Do this spell to help attract or pick the right couples therapist.

On the orange candle write "couples therapist" or write the name of a specific therapist if you have already made this decision. If you perform the spell with a specific therapist in mind, you can insure that this particular counselor will be effective. Write the names of the couple on the pink candle. Sprinkle a circle of dill, caraway, and parsnip around the two candles. If you are using fresh dill, you should shred it into small pieces. The same with the parsnip. Use equal amounts and make the circle at least half an inch thick. Light the orange candle with a match and then light the pink candle from the orange candle's flame. Meditate upon your situation in front of the burning candles. See you and your mate benefiting greatly from the work in the therapist's office. If you or your partner feel reluctant to go for counseling, you can also sprinkle lime juice over the pink candle to add influence to the spell. In this case, use two separate pink candles. The candle for the reluctant party should be anointed with lime juice, and the other pink candle will be unanointed with the willing party's name. If both are reluctant or afraid, use one pink candle with both names on it and anoint with lime juice. Burn these candles until they are extinguished. You may blow them out and relight them, but at some point they should completely finish burning. When they are done, you will gather up all the melted wax and herbs and form into a ball. Place in a plastic bag and bring to your therapist's office to add healing power to your session.

PHONE SPELL REVISITED

Ingredients:

> **black pepper and sage**
> **lemon juice**
> **pine oil**
> **rosebud**
> **cotton ball**
> **tinfoil**

fennel seeds
oregano
dill and caraway seeds

Since the release of my first book, *Supermarket Sorceress,* I have received phone calls, letters, and faxes from all around the world. Most calls were to thank me, and occasionally I was asked for additional help. The spell most talked about, and the only one with inconsistent reports in achieving success, was the phone spell. Initially this surprised me, as I have suggested this spell for years and my clients have been quite satisfied with their results. A reporter for *The New York Times* even wrote about the spell. After working it, she received not a phone call, but a fax, from the gentleman in question.

This disparity puzzled me for many months until I received a phone call from Belinda. She had been working the phone spell for three weeks with no results. Carlos had not called her. Upon further questioning, she revealed to me that the last communication with Carlos had been on the day she threw him out of the house. She whacked him repeatedly over the head with a cast-iron skillet and told him to never darken her door again.

"Belinda," I said. "Listen, honey, you're gonna need more than a phone spell to get this guy to communicate. Let's start by healing his head and healing your heart."

After this conversation I investigated the other failed cases, and it turned out each had ended the last communication with an argument. There was only one situation where the phone spell did work. Roger's ex-fiancée finally called him up to say: "F—— off!" Poor Roger.

The following is a new spell combining love healing with communication. Black pepper and sage can be used to dispel anger. Lemon, pine, and rose are used for healing the mind, body, and heart. You are going to incorporate these new ingredients with the traditional phone spell ingredients. Hold a piece of cotton in your lap and shape it into the initial of the person you want to call. Lay the cotton on a piece of tinfoil. Sprinkle a quarter teaspoon each of black pepper and sage on the cotton.

Squeeze three drops of lemon juice and three drops of pine oil onto the cotton. Crush one dried rosebud over it. Now continue on with the original spell. Sprinkle a circle of equal amounts of fennel, oregano, dill, and caraway seeds around the cotton. Carefully fold the tinfoil into a square. Tinfoil will add an extra dose of attraction to your Mercurial herbs. Place the foil pouch underneath or next to the phone.

"Give it a while, Belinda. At least another three weeks."

LOVE ON THE ROCKS

"CANDY IS DANDY, BUT LIQUOR IS QUICKER" SPELL

Ingredients:

> **orange-flavored vodka**
> **sprig of fresh mint**
> **lots of ice (rocks)**
> **sweet vermouth**
> **slice of lime (optional)**

Alcohol was and still is used by many religions to induce a state of ecstasy. Today, in churches consecrated wine symbolizes the blood of Christ. In the ancient Eleusinian rites wine was symbolic of the blood of Dionysus. Orgiastic rites of ecstasy were performed after consuming alcoholic substances. I don't think I have to further explain the magical principle behind this spell. Ogden Nash said it so well in the borrowed title. Consuming alcohol can quickly induce sexual euphoria. But just for those die-hards, I will explain the magical properties of each ingredient.

Sweet vermouth is made of red wine and a secret blend of herbs. Vermouth induces unbridled passion. Vodka, because it is odorless and colorless, is considered invisible magic. "Slip a Mickey" magic, if you will. (Note: Bad karma to do alcohol magic on a sober subject!) If you use orange-flavored vodka, you are bringing the element of love into the formula. Orange blossom is considered the flower and fruit of heart bumping. If you are interested only in bumping below the belt, please do not use orange. Substitute straight vodka or any berry vodka, as this will produce only sexual feelings. Mint, ruled by Mars, is the herb of lust. Orange and mint are a hot combination in any form. Use a slice of lime if you feel you need an extra push to get over shyness. Lime is considered a commanding, compelling formula. The ice, of course, is to freeze any reserve your partner may have about having sex with you. This spell is pretty straightforward. Rinse out two glasses with sweet vermouth. Add vodka to a shaker full of ice, shake vigorously while imagining your desire coming to fruition. When you have the completed picture in your mind, pour the chilled vodka into the glasses. Add a sprig of mint and a slice of lime (optional), make a sexy, slutty toast, and serve.

LOVE UNCROSSING I

Ingredients:

> **ammonia**
> **celery**
> **salt**

The first type of love uncrossing is to remove obstacles to finding love in your life. This spell is designed for those who keep meeting Mr. or Ms. Wrong. The magic of the spell is to remove undesirables from your path. The spell can also remove qualities within you that block you from giving and receiving love. On a new moon, place a drop of ammonia into a tub full of water. Bathe in this water. Ammonia is one of the strongest uncrossers. When you get out of the tub, go into the kitchen and wash three stalks of celery. Lay the first stalk down with its spine touching the counter. Lay the second stalk across it (with the spine facing you) to form a cross. Cut the third stalk into quarters by making a vertical slice down the center and a horizontal slice through the center. Arrange these four smaller pieces in between the four angles of the cross so that you have now formed an X within the cross. You will end up with eight points. This is a very old voodoo *veve** used to uncross the roads and remove obstacles from your path.

Surround this *veve* with a circle of salt. Salt is an excellent agent of purification. Celery was eaten in Rome to increase sexual attraction. It is ruled by Mercury, so it can help to open the channels of love. Let this sit on your altar (see ''Love Altars'') for fifteen to twenty minutes. Look at the veve and see yourself unblocked in love. Rub each piece in the salt and ingest to remove obstacles in your love life.

LOVE UNCROSSING II

Ingredients:

> **ammonia**
> **salt**
> **rosewater or rosebuds**

The second love uncrossing is used to remove problems within a relationship. This spell will help to unblock a couple so that they may move forward instead of breaking

*A *veve* is a magical symbol usually drawn on the ground, written on parchment, or carved into candles.

up. On the new moon you must both wash your floors down with water, a half capful of ammonia, and a capful of rosewater or three rosebuds. If you have carpeting, prepare this mixture in a spray bottle and mist all rooms. As soon as you can see the first sliver of a new moon light in the sky (usually one to two nights after the new moon), go to the crossroads together. You both must throw salt over your left shoulders to banish any warring between you. On the stroke of midnight, you must kiss at the crossroads.

MARITAL MENDER

Ingredients:

> **a blender**
> **heavy cream**
> **cling peaches**
> **strawberries**
> **cherries**

This is a soothing concoction that can promote forgiveness after a marital spat. It should be consumed shortly after an argument. You can also make this potion as a preventive if you feel the air getting thick and sense a quarrel is about to begin. All the ingredients are soothing lunar and Mother Goddess foods. Peaches and cream are emotional cleansers, so drowsiness may occur as the negative energy is drained out. Strawberries on their own can ignite the passions, but combined with peaches and cream, they protect love in a relationship. Don't expect this drink to induce passion. It will probably make you both sleepy, which is as good a way as any to stop a fight.

Fill a blender with heavy cream, peaches, and strawberries. Let it whirl and visualize the two of you becoming unified, no longer divided by your differences. You may also add a little honey or sugar to sweeten your attitudes toward each other. Pour ingredients into two bowls and top each with a cherry. Do not leave out the cherries. It is never good to empty a space of negative energy without refilling the space with positive energy. The cherries are for self-love and happiness. After a spat, it is important to give your partner a gift of inner confidence so he or she will feel safe enough to extend love to you once again.

SPELL FOR RESOLVE AND ACTION

Ingredients:

   **carrots
   scallions
   spinach**

Do you have something you need to do? Is your relationship rocky because you've put that something on the back burner for way too long? Maybe you need to find a bigger apartment or to lose weight. Perhaps you've been putting off having a baby, and now the internal clock's alarm is about to ring. It may be going for counseling, or calling your in-laws and telling them you are not coming for Christmas this year. Whatever the situation—even if it is that you have to split up and need the resolve to leave—this spell will enable you to take the actions necessary to save yourself or your relationship.

On a Tuesday, the day of feisty, active Mars, lay out some carrots, raw spinach, and scallions on your kitchen counter. Scallions are good for getting rid of obstacles. Slowly peel away the outer layers from the scallion and state the obstacles that are keeping you from achieving your goal. As you peel the carrot name all the small steps you must take to fulfill your goal. Take three fresh leaves of spinach. Wash them and hold them in your hands. Rub them swiftly between your palms and visualize yourself having the strength to take these steps and complete your task. Finally, hold a whole scallion, a carrot stick, and a spinach leaf in your right hand and eat together to give yourself an internal push to take action.

STONE CIRCLE OF LOVE SPELL

Ingredients:

seven rocks or stones

Rocks are definitely available at the beach, and it is most magical if you can collect them on your own property. Witches believe that Stonehenge and other ancient sites are very powerful places. A circle of stones is a spot the goddess is sure to enter.

If you want to bless, protect, and empower your relationship, stand in a sacred circle of stones with your lover. You can also collect seven (the number of love) small rocks and arrange them in a circle on your altar. Place a picture of the two of you in this circle or make an XXX for Kisses talisman and place it in the circle of rocks.

SPELL TO SAVE YOUR MARRIAGE FROM DIVORCE

Ingredients:

peas
capers
onions
butter or olive oil

This spell is to assist you in hanging in there and not taking the easy route out. Onions are purifying. I recommend pearl onions for this spell to help you uncover the layer of preciousness remaining in your union. Onions belong to both Mercury (the communicator) and Mars (the fighter). In this case the fight would be to save the marriage by learning to communicate. The onion is a bastion against evil. It can spiritually cleanse the most difficult hurts and betrayals. Arabs in medieval times recommended onions for stimulating sexual desire.

The caper, a multifaceted magical bud, is considered primarily an aphrodisiac. It holds the sexy scent of its romantic origins, the Mediterranean, within its core. It is also considered a philosophical or wise food, said to bring insight, promote nostalgic feelings, and assist lost souls in coming home. All pickled foods belong to Saturn or Capricorn, the sign of hard and committed work. Saturn can be a separator, but she can also empower and turn bitter experiences into gems of wisdom. The peas, of course, represent peace. They are ruled by the gentle loving and healing planetary force of Venus. The combination of these three foods connect the heart (pea), the groin (onion), and the mind/spirit (caper). If the problems leading to your divorce were caused by money, add extra capers and peas. All green foods can heal money problems.

Sauté the onions and peas with a small amount of butter or olive oil. Visualize all the difficulties between you softening. Butter and olive oil are both used to nurture, heal, bless, and protect. Allow the relationship to be cleansed and ask the goddess for help in approaching things with love and peace from this point on. As you stir in the capers, try to remember the high spots of the marriage. Devise a plan or caper to bring you back to that point in time. Eat warm with your partner if the relationship feels chilly and you need to rekindle the passion. Eat chilled with your partner to relieve tension if things have become too heated and argumentative. *Never eat luke-warm.* The spell will lose its effectiveness, as will your marriage!

HOT ICE SPELL

Ingredients:

an ice cube tray (in pink, if possible)
vanilla extract
ground cardamom seed
rosewater
naranja en flor **(dried orange peel)**

There is a small bathhouse tucked away in the folds of Toronto where magic happens. I have taken an oath never to disclose its exact location. It is a special bathhouse for women only. If you are of the female persuasion, you can go there and have your whole body pampered in very unusual ways. A tiny woman who looks like a cross between a geisha girl and a mermaid will walk on your back, scrub you down with salts and herbs, mix you magical potions to drink, anoint you from head to toe with scented oils, and massage every inch of your being. She will also show you catalogs filled with unthinkable and delicious erotic sex toys.

She will take you into a beautifully tiled steamroom and sit with you until you are so hot, you can hardly stand it. Then she will magically manifest a bowl filled with specially prepared ice cubes. She will make you beg for the ice, and then she will insert the cubes into places on your body where you never even imagined putting ice. You will swear you have entered the "ice"lestial realms.

Then, if she likes you, she will take you out to dinner and then dancing. You will become aware that you are more attractive than usual, as many people flirt with you on the dance floor. It is then she reveals that the ice cubes are filled with a magic love potion. She tells you this potion is double strength. You realize she is telling the truth when at the end of the evening you bring back not one, but two beautiful lovers to your hotel room.

Take a pink ice tray and sprinkle ground cardamom seeds and dried orange peel into each section. They should be of a very find grind. Place two drops of vanilla extract and seven drops of rosewater into each section. Fill all to the brim with water. Place in freezer. Use to invoke a steamy night.

TROUBLESHOOTING AND TECHNICALITIES

"OR BETTER" SPELL

At Enchantments, the occult/goddess shop where I received my witch training, we have two very magical words that we add to all love spells: ''or better.'' The ''or better'' insures that you will not make a mistake and through your stubborn will draw an unsuitable partner to be chained to your side for unhappily ever after. ''Or better'' says that you would like to love so and so, but you trust the gods to deliver whoever is best for you. ''Or better'' is a way out, a loophole in love.

Working the ''Or Better'' Spell is very simple. Just add these two magical words after the person's name and sign that you are working on. In traditional love spells, one always adds the sign of the person next to his/her name. It is a magical form of identification, and a spell is known to work better by adding the astrological signs of all parties involved. Some spells require chanting a name; if so, also chant ''or better.''

If a spell requires carving a name into a candle or fruit, or tracing initials on an object, you will trace or carve these words as well. For example, you will carve ''John Sagittarius (or better)'' into your apple or candle. See how easy!*

Be forewarned that using the ''Or Better'' Spell does require complete open-mindedness and trust in the deities of love. You may not receive at all what you had

---

*Never carve ''John John Sagittarius (or better),'' as even the gods can't do better than a Kennedy!

in mind, but you will receive what works best for you. Case in point: Venus* always thought Pluto* was a handsome devil. Unfortunately, Pluto was married to her best friend, Persephone.* When Persephone and Pluto got divorced (by the way, he got everything and she had to move back home with Mother), Venus (after a respectable turn of season) decided to cast a love spell on her best friend's ex-man. Trusting the gods, she carved the name and sign "Pluto Scorpio," followed by the magical verse "or better," into a ripe pomegranate. She ate three seeds, and in three days' time, Pluto came to her. After spending one night together in the underworld of love, Venus realized her handsome devil was a horrid beast—a boar (and a bore in bed to boot). She ran crying to her trusted friend, Persephone, and after commiserating over their bad choice in men, they found themselves laughing, frolicking, and rolling in the hay. They remain happily together to this very day. Who woulda thunk it?

LOVE AND GEOGRAPHY SPELL

Ingredients:

atlas or map
pink taper candles
orange, white, and red tacks or pushpins
cinnamon chewing gum (cinnamon and acacia)
hot chili pepper oil (optional)

This spell is to draw together two lovers who are presently living in different cities. If you know which one needs to make the move, begin by putting the first pushpin in the city of that person (person A). This pushpin should be orange or red: these are colors of movement and action. Make a trail of red and orange pushpins from city A

*Witch names used to protect identity.

to city B. Surround city B (the place you want person A to end up in) with a circle of white pushpins. This will create white light around the aura of this city.

Place two pink taper candles within the circle of white pushpins (be sure to make your circle wide enough). Carve person A's name on one candle and person B's name on the other candle. Let them burn side by side and melt into one another. Keep the map out and continue burning candles weekly until the mission is accomplished. To speed things up, anoint the red and orange pushpins with hot chili pepper oil.

If you want a faraway lover to communicate with you, lay a map upon your altar and chew a piece of cinnamon gum. Take the gum from your mouth and stretch it from the city that he/she is in to the city that you are in. Cinnamon gum contains acacia. Witches use acacia for love, binding, and communication spells. Combined with cinnamon, it brings swift communication in love and is known to deliver billet-doux across the miles.

TO KEEP A LOVER FAITHFUL

Ingredients:

> **footprint in the dirt**
> **clipping of a bedsheet**
> **small whisk broom or matchbook or index card**
> **sterilized needle and red thread**

To perform this spell, you must obtain two very important ingredients. The first is a footprint in the dirt from your lover's right shoe. This is necessary to head (and keep) your lover in the right direction. The second item is a small clipping from a bedsheet (unlaundered) upon which you have made passionate love to each other. Cut a square four inches by four inches. This will be a sympathetic magical link to your love. The remaining items will vary depending upon the nature of your relationship.

Take a small whisk broom or even a matchbook or index card and scrape up the footprint made in the dirt. If you find this impossible to obtain, I recommend the following: Dust the bathroom floor with talcum powder while your lover is in the shower. When he or she steps out, you will have a footprint. Sweep it up and save as soon as possible. Bare footprints are actually more potent than shoeprints because they capture the *sole* of your partner.

Another method is to take a pair of your lover's favorite, most worn shoes (shoes that contain his or her essence) and obtain the print yourself by placing your right hand in the right shoe and then pressing the shoe in the dirt. This must be done using dirt from the crossroads. A crossroads is any place where two streets intersect and the road continues on in all four directions for at least eight blocks without obstruction.

Once you have obtained the footprint you must sprinkle it over the bedsheet clipping while chanting these words:

> *Stay at home do not roam*
> *You are mine. My Lover*
> *Do not take another*
> *Walk my way, every day.*

Repeat this verse three times and then carefully roll up the fabric with the footprint inside.

This ritual must be completed at midnight on a full moon. It is best to begin your preparations on the new moon, thus giving you about two and a half weeks to gather your footprint and get your sheets—well, I'll leave the sheets to your imagination. On the full moon take a sterilized needle and red thread. Prick your left thumb with the needle and anoint the thread with your blood. This will lend enormous power to the spell. Thread the needle and sew the open ends of the sheet square closed.

Now stand on the talisman you have created and repeat the verse three more times. Hold the talisman between your thighs and squeeze. Imagine your lover locked in your embrace. Move the talisman over your heart, open that center, and send love to your partner. Press it against your throat and visualize good communication between you and your partner. Kiss the talisman with your lips and then place it under the mattress to insure fidelity.

A'MAIZE'N LOVER SPELL

Ingredients:

    corn on the cob
    olive oil

Yunax* is the ancient Mayan corn god: god of the mount and the mountain. Most of us can imagine what a woman might do with a corncob and a palmful of olive oil, but this spell is actually designed for a man. If you are unhappy with the size of your penis, obtain a corncob that would represent the stature of your dreams. Anoint it with olive oil, stand it up on an altar, and meditate for several minutes. Pray to Yunax not for a larger phallus, but rather to become master of the mount. If you already have a partner, this means the magic is to make a better fit. If you do not have a partner, the prayer is to attract someone who will be a perfect fit. I have seen miraculous changes as a result of this spell. Remember, guys, it's not the meat, it's the motion. Yunax will teach you the art of scaling the walls and reaching the summit successfully. Work this spell to make your member godlike.

*Pronounced Un-kash.

SPELL FOR IMPOTENCE

Ingredients:

> **whole garlic**
> **purple onions**
> **toasted sesame oil**
> **oysters**

The Talmud, a compilation of rabbinical observations from the fifth and sixth centuries, mentions garlic as a good food for male virility. Medieval Arab texts call for onions to keep a man's member strong. I recommend using both garlic and onions. Sesame oil comes from seeds. Traditionally all foods that have numerous seeds are good for curing impotence. Sesame is also sacred to that ever-rising god of the sun, Apollo. Oysters are a sacred sexual food that hold the power and mystery of male and female seduction within their folds.

Rub a whole garlic with toasted sesame oil. Cut two purple onions into quarters and rub them with the oil as well. Wrap garlic in tinfoil and roast in the oven for forty-five minutes. Open the foil and place the quartered onions next to the roasted garlic. Broil for seven more minutes. Remove and let cool slightly, then feed to your man. Roasting or broiling is a way to quickly bring up the juices of a meat. As the man eats the onions and garlic, it will create heat in his own body—not necessarily a sexual heat, but a physical/alchemical heat. Let him pull the garlic apart with his hands and suck the butter out of the skin of each clove. Finally, you must anoint the phallus with warm oysters. Continue rubbing until heat is created and an erection occurs. It is good to also anoint the penis with your mouth. The combination of saliva and oyster juice is said to be intoxicating and believed to prolong stiffness. (If this feels uncomfortable to you, place the oyster in your mouth first and anoint it with saliva before rubbing it on the penis.) If, within a half hour, no erection has occurred, let the man rest and repeat this ritual after three hours' time. If you still have no success, wait another three days and then repeat. *Note: This spell is not a substitute for seeking medical attention. Diseases such as diabetes can cause impotence and should be treated medically. This spell can be quite effective in removing spiritual and psychological blocks causing impotence. Please feel free to be creative with this ritual and incorporate his personal sexual fantasy into the spell.*

SPELL TO BRING ON FEMALE ORGASM

Ingredients:

> **figs**
> **pralines (or pecans or almonds and sugar)**
> **apricot**
> **carob (or chocolate) powder**

Before I begin to explain this spell, I have just one piece of advice for women who are unable to achieve orgasms with their partners—I specify "with their partners," because I doubt you bother doing this naughty thing on your own. *Stop faking it!*

The ingredients here combine foods of self-love, self-confidence, trust, sexual stimulants, and communication. Figs represent the vagina. They are very sexual and can promote self-love and self-knowledge in women. The praline, made by browning pecans or almonds in boiling sugar, was named after the Frenchman Praslin, whose chef invented it. *La praline* is also French slang for the clitoris. Using figs and pralines together in a spell will promote clitoral as well as vaginal orgasm. Apricots and carob powder, which are ruled by the sign of Libra, promote trust between partners. You may substitute chocolate, as it is an aphrodisiac, but carob has the added attributes of creating relaxation, communication, and trust.

You can bathe in these ingredients before meeting your lover. You may let your lover bathe you in them as a prelude to lovemaking. When you bathe, the skin, the largest organ in the body, absorbs the ingredients very quickly. The bath infuses the aura as well. Eating requires digestion, which takes a bit longer. Just keep this in mind. Best not to guzzle this down your throat ten minutes before you are about to have sex and expect it to work. You must ingest these foods a day or two before making love.

BEES' KNEES—A WHOLE LOT OF HONEY SPELLS

HONEY LOVE SPELLS

My favorite witch, BroomHilda, says, "There ain't nothin' you can't do with honey."
Bees are considered the messengers of the gods. They deliver the prayers of humanity
to the heavenly realms. All products connected with bees have magical powers (beeswax, honey, pollen, royal jelly, propolis . . .). It is believed that any bee product can
hold and deliver a magical message or prayer. Known as the magical elixir of the
gods, honey is often given as an offering to love goddesses. Its sweet and sticky
nature symbolizes the type of love the petitioner wishes the goddess to deliver. There
is a custom of tasting the honey first, which stems from an incident that occurred with
the Yoruban goddess Oshun. Someone tried to poison her with honey, so as a result
we always taste all offerings to insure that they are safe. The following are an as-
sortment of honey love spells, all designed to be delivered with a sting.

HONEY ONE

Ingredients:

honey

It is said that Cleopatra bathed in honey. Many beauty products contain honey, and it can be used magically to enhance your own beauty. You can make a facial or coat your whole body in honey while calling on the Yoruban goddess Oshun, queen of sexuality and beauty. Do not soap off the honey unless you have a bar soap made of pure olive oil. The combination of honey and olive oil can increase sexual stamina, and the Romans believed it made one more attractive. If you do not have pure olive oil soap, let the honey just melt off your body under warm water. Leaving a scent or slight residue can be very sexy when you encounter someone up close.

On a new moon, get in the tub or shower and anoint your whole body completely with honey. As you do this, call out all the qualities you would like to enhance in yourself and all the qualities you would like to attract in another person. Leave the honey on for three minutes, then rinse off with warm water and air dry. This ritual will draw someone who is sweet to love you.

This ritual is also recommended for couples who are very much in love. In fact, they love each other so much that they have an irrational fear of losing each other. Honey has the magical property of opening the memory to past lives. Perhaps this fear stems from a past life in which you really did lose each other. This honey spell can help you remember the source of this fear, while at the same time insuring that your love sticks.

Anoint each other with honey from head to toe. Actually start from the center of the belly and work your way up. Then start from the center of the belly and work your way down. After you have both been anointed, hug each other tightly for three minutes. During this time state and chant all the reasons why you love each other and want to stick together. After three minutes shower down or rinse in warm bathwater.

HONEY TWO

Ingredients:

> **honey**
> **peanuts or peanut butter**

Peanuts are a prosperity food, but they are also known as the hardworking nut. Honey and peanuts can be used for two purposes. First, they can bless a union with prosperity. The combination should be used if money is a problem affecting the relationship. Honey and peanuts can also be used to sweeten your attitude toward the hard work that is needed to make your relationship work. It is a good formula to use when sacrifices are necessary and to make you or your partner happy to undergo such sacrifices.

No, I am not going to ask you to smear peanut butter all over your body! Simply eat these foods together or make a peanut-butter-and-honey sand*witch* on oat bread and split it with your partner.

HONEY THREE

Ingredients:

> **honey**
> **olive oil**
> **sea salt**

Honey, olive oil, and sea salt are the three magical staples of life. To keep a relationship pure, uncrossed, and sweetly primed for the future, mix in a large bowl a half pound of sea salt, half a cup of olive oil, and a tablespoonful of honey.* The

*Measurements are per person.

honey and olive oil will make you more attractive to yourselves and to each other.
The salt will remove any negative energy that has accumulated between you. The
lovers should massage and scrub each other down with this mixture. Follow up by
showering together (no soap, please). Then anoint all pulse points with honey. Make
it into a magical sensual game. If you do this once a month, the magic will always
remain in your relationship!

If you are single, you can perform this spell on yourself for purification and to clear
the way for a new relationship. In this case it is easier to take a bath with three fistfuls
of sea salt, half a cup of olive oil, and a spoonful of honey to a tub of bathwater.
Bring in a loofah sponge and give yourself a good scrub in the tub. When you emerge
from the tub, anoint all pulse points with honey.

SPELL FOR BEA

Ingredients:

   beeswax
   honey
   honeycomb
   dried mushroom
   rosebud
   mint
   nutmeg
   chamomile teabag
   cardamom seed
   an almond

Beatrice has been a darling friend of mine for years. She works on Wall Street,
although she doesn't have to. Beatrice was born with a golden spoon. She has every-

thing but love. Love and devotion. Complete and utter slavish devotion. That is what Beatrice requires of her man. Believe me, I know. She tells me twenty times a day.

"I want him to obsess over me. Why isn't he obsessing over me?" she whines.

Because he probably read Section 13 of this book, I think to myself. I answer: "Well, Beatrice, have you been practicing that helium balloon technique that I taught you?"

"No. I've been too busy thinking about him," she replies.

"Beatrice, I told you, you've got to gather all your thoughts about him in a big imaginary helium balloon. Then let go the string of your thoughts. Let the balloon float away into the clouds, and then eventually it will light upon his head. Then he will be obsessed with thoughts of you."

"I can't do it. I just can't do it. Why don't you fix me some more of those red skull candles?" she begged.

"I'm all out. Besides, you told me they stopped working."

"Well, maybe they'll work again."

As you can see, she's nonnegotiable. That's why she's so filthy rich. But when it comes to love Beatrice is lost. She doesn't have a clue. Not only that, she once confided to me that she fakes her orgasms. Oh, Beatrice, what am I to do with you?

I prepared a special satchel for Beatrice to carry in her corset. It contained a drop of beeswax from a candle, a drop of honey, and a piece of a raw honeycomb. You see, Beatrice is like a queen bee. She wants the type of mate who will die for her love. The pouch also contained a dried mushroom to increase her glamour. I placed a thought in the mushroom to create an illusion over Beatrice as well. You see, the man really did love her, but for Beatrice it was never enough. I asked the mushroom to make Beatrice believe he was truly devoted.

A rosebud, a pinch of mint, and a nutmeg were added, for it is said that no one can hide the truth around these herbs. This way Beatrice would not be able to fake a thing. I included a chamomile teabag to relax her. Last, I added a cardamom seed and an almond to make sure that she truly would be sexually gratified. I have not heard from her for a while, so I guess all must be well. Or at least better. Believe me, she paid a pretty penny for this spell. The price alone should have shut her up!

HONEY AND WINE SPELL

Viva il vino spumeggiante
Nel bicchiere scintillante,
Come il riso dell'amante
Mite infonde il giubilo!

—*Cavalleria Rusticana* (Mascagni)

Wine is a substance of ecstasy, "bringing happiness, like a lover's smile." Honey and wine both are considered precious gifts of the gods. This is a very spiritual/tantric formula used to bond a couple sexually and spiritually and to create a divine energy or a divine offspring between them. Anointing is a sacred ritual of witches. It is done before any magical rite or initiation. Anointing is traditionally done with oil. Honey and wine are sometimes used as well. Anointing with honey and wine would be done to prepare yourself for union with the god and goddess. In marriage rites two strangers are joined in a holy union. Their blood is made one. This magical task is done by binding their souls together with the thread of divinity. Wine is the male aspect of divinity, and honey is the female aspect. Both are often used as a substitute for blood. The act of creating a child also combines the blood of two bodies into one. If we combine egg and seed with honey and wine, we conceive a divine as well as an earthly progeny. In ancient Greece there are many myths about men and women who have been parented by a god. Helen and Hercules were fathered by Zeus. Theseus had two fathers, one a mortal king and the other the god Poseidon.

"Two fathers? How can this be?" you ask.

The concept of "son or daughter of God" is much older than the Jesus, Mary, and Joseph tale. Virgin births were very common in ancient pagan times. In some cases, an anonymous man or a man of low caste was used as the sperm donor. Then the child was considered to be fathered only by the god. If, however, the male donor was a king or of royal lineage, then he shared the position of father with the god. The priestess would prepare herself ritually, a man would be chosen, and the god would be drawn down into him. Then he and the priestess would couple. The offspring of that coupling would be considered half human and half divine. In modern Wicca, the priest and priestess will often invoke the god and goddess into each other before mating. Not only offspring, but all sexual energy raised is considered a form of divine ecstasy. If you would like to make love with your partner as god/goddess, god/god, or goddess/goddess, you must anoint each other's lips, breasts, genitals, knees, and feet with honey and wine on a full moon before making love. Then anoint each area with your lips to draw the god or goddess into your bodies. If a child is conceived during this union, he or she will be sublime and divine.

Because the combination of honey and wine is used to attain spiritual heights, it can also be used by a single person who wants to practice celibacy. In this case, anoint your pulse points on a new moon and you will find strength in your vows and a surge of celestial power and energy fill your body. This is also the spell for women who wish to parent by parthenogenesis. In such a case, do the spell on a blue moon.

HONEY DEW SPELL

Ingredients:

> honey
> melon

To bless a family and to create more love among all individuals, anoint a whole cantaloupe or honeydew melon with honey and leave it at the seashore as an offering to Yemaya. Yemaya is the ocean mother, and she rules the hearth and home. In other traditions of magic, melons are used as a seduction formula to win someone already committed to another. To work this spell, cut a melon in half and place a piece of paper in one half with the name of the person you desire. Pour a generous amount of honey over the paper and into the melon half. Cover up the melon with the second half and keep in a dark place (under the bed is good) for a new moon to a full moon. The melon should become moldy for the spell to be activated. On the full moon, bury the whole melon or place at the crossroads. Call out the name of the person you desire as you do so.

HONEY STEW

Ingredients:

> **potatoes**
> **flanken meat**
> **kidney beans, white beans, navy beans**
> **barley**
> **onion**
> **salt**
> **honey**

Cholent is a special stew made on the Jewish Sabbath. One source tells me that the cholent reflects the guests and will be only as good as the dinner company. Another source tells me that the cholent reflects the merits of the family at whose home it is served. In Jewish tradition the Sabbath is considered the Queen or the Bride of God. Therefore any food consumed on the Sabbath has special merit—goddess merit, if you will.

After having examined the magical components, I concluded that cholent is indeed a magic stew for love. Potatoes are ruled by the moon and are a food of compassion and nurturing. They also have the ability to absorb any negative energy. Meat, especially beef, is sacred to the love goddess Hathor, the Egyptian equivalent of Venus. Meat also represents grounding and prosperity and brings an awareness of our connection to the physical plane. Meat represents both physical protection and sensuality. Beans were fed to the gods in ancient Egypt and are considered a very spiritual food. They are also believed to increase the sexual appetite and impregnate women, which is why Saint Jerome forbade his nuns to eat them. Barley was considered a food of fertility and prosperity in ancient Egypt, Sumeria, India, Babylonia, and China. Onions are for cleansing and healing, and according to Arab lore, they increase male sexual potency. Salt is a purifier and protector, and honey is that super love glue that binds together all these blessed foods.

The last magical element of cholent is the way in which it is cooked. You must slow-cook it for at least sixteen hours. Traditionally it is prepared on Friday evenings before sundown. All the ingredients are mixed together in a pot and brought to a boil. The dish is then covered and placed on a low flame on a stove top or in the oven. The dish is then served the following afternoon for lunch. I recommend cooking the cholent in the oven, as this is considered the womb of the goddess. Invite a potential lover over for lunch, and if the cholent turns out good, well then, rest assured that your lunch guest is worth pursuing. In accordance with my second source, cholent should be served to the whole family to promote *shalom bi'yit* (peace in the home); also to remove any negativity and to promote longevity, love, prosperity, and future generations.

FIRE OF LOVE SPELL

Ingredients:

> **honey**
> **wax**

Honey and wax are doubly *bee*witching, as both are made from bees. Take a red or pink candle and anoint with honey to draw someone to you. Carve both your names into the candle and surround the names with a heart. Burn on the new moon to attract a new lover or on a full moon to strengthen a relationship that is already in progress. Burn a white candle anointed with honey if you want to heal a relationship. This is best done on a new moon. The honey will sweeten the wounds and the burning wax will purify any surrounding negativity and seal in the white light and protective vibrations of love.

THESMOPHORIA SPELL

The ancient Greeks made special cakes out of honey and sesame to honor the rites of the goddesses Kore and Demeter. The festival of their rites was called the Thesmophoria and could be attended only by women (and some clever drag queens).

I have seen hard candies in the supermarket made of sesame and honey. You may also use sesame crackers and spread honey on them. Eat these on a new or full moon to learn and share more about women's mysteries. Two women can also share these cakes to create a mystical and sexual union between them.

LOVE PETITION TO OSHUN

Thanks to H. Ferrer, sister of Oshun, for sharing this spell

Ingredients:

honey
five oranges

five eggs whites
cinnamon
five pennies
five pieces of yellow paper with petitions
jasmine rice
coconut flakes
cake sprinkles
a mirror (in a gold frame, if possible)

Oshun is one of the most sensual and powerful love goddesses. She is a sophisticated lady as well as a precocious little girl. It is customary to offer her lavish gifts in exchange for her help (although it is also customary to give her something up front and promise her something else once she grants your request). She has been known to take offerings and simply overlook why the gifts were given. Yet she never forgets the promise of a reward to come. Oshun is a goddess who loves to cut a deal. Practitioners of Santeria keep elaborate altars to Oshun and feed these altars constantly. So upon first introduction to this popular Yoruban queen, you had better prepare something special to attract her attention.

Oshun loves a mirror. Each of the Orishas* (there are seven) has a special tool. Oshun's mirror is the pool of wisdom and reflects her infinite beauty. Begin by placing a large mirror on an altar or table. The rest of the ingredients are all things that Oshun loves. Prepare them as follows and place upon the mirror to draw her to your side. Begin by spreading a circle of coconut flakes around the outer edge of the mirror. This is actually for Ellegua, the remover of obstacles. Protocol dictates that you speak to Ellegua before approaching any of the other Orishas. Now you are ready to call upon Oshun. Take five oranges, hollow them out, and arrange inside the circle of coconut flakes. Taste some honey on your thumb and then place a generous portion

*Yoruban gods and goddesses.

in each hollowed-out orange. Sprinkle a teaspoon of cinnamon on top of the honey. Sprinkle ten grains of uncooked jasmine rice in each orange.

At this point, you have done enough preliminary buttering up to ask something of Oshun. Take five small squares of yellow paper and write five wishes or requests for love. Make five folds in each paper and place one request in each orange. Drop a penny on top of each request. Now for the *pièce de résistance*. You will beat five egg whites until you have created a fluffy meringue. (Be careful: if you beat too long, your meringue will turn watery!) As you beat the eggs, concentrate upon your requests or upon the image of Oshun, or both. Scoop the meringue into the oranges and fill them completely. The meringue should sit like balls of ice cream on top of the oranges. Dust the meringue with multicolored sugar cake sprinkles to complete the dish.

Leave this altar in place from a new moon to a full moon. If mold appears, that is a sign that Oshun is eating the offering. On the Sunday after the full moon, take all but the mirror to the closest river and drop in the water. All rivers are the home of Oshun. Save the mirror for future communication with Oshun. By the way, if you decide to promise her more goodies after she grants your wishes, just remember— her number is five or multiples of five, and she loves all things yellow, copper, and gold. Fans and peacock feathers really turn her on!

Soul Mates

PUCK'S LOVE SPELL, OR THE PARIS PLOT UNDONE

Ingredients:

eight turkey wings
an umbrella with eight spokes

Alexander is one of my regular clients. Alex always requires what I call high-maintenance magic. Whenever Alex falls in love (and he falls hard and often), the operative word is "unavailable." I am never surprised when he shows up in complete desperation at my door. This time he was despondent over a certain Helen. Even I had to admit that this Helen was a fine specimen of a woman, of a much higher caliber than Alexander's usual suspects. There were, however, complications. Helen was madly in love and completely obsessed with a cruel and cocky Frenchman. Of course, the Frenchman had used her up and dumped her as fast as yesterday's trash. But Helen still thought of him night and day. To complicate matters even further, Helen was married to a very strong and insanely jealous Armenian named Manny.

The whole situation made my third eye throb.

"My goddess, Alexander. Couldn't you have fallen in love with someone less complicated? Like Madonna?"

"No. I love Helen. She is my soul mate. I will not, I cannot, rest until she is mine.

I will do anything, Lady Venus,'' he said, turning up his wrists and offering them to me.

"Oh please, Alex. This too shall pass. She's not worth killing yourself over,'' I said.

"Killing myself? I had no such thoughts. I imagined you might want some of my blood to make the spell more powerful,'' he said, making a fist and flexing his veins.

"No, thank you. But you wouldn't happen to have some aspirin?'' I asked.

"No, sorry,'' he said, and then went into one of his melancholy stares. The poor man has been seen walking the streets of New York in this sort of daze for days. To his credit, this obsession with Helen seemed to be more constant than it was with all the other girls. He had been having recurring dreams about her on and off for the past two years. Finally he felt it was time to act, which was why he had come to me.

My third eye wasn't feeling any better. Should I work a spell to relieve obsession on Alex? (That spell never seems to work on him anyway.) How about trying that on Helen? Or should we just do a separation spell for her? But whom shall I separate her from? The Frenchman or the Armenian? Maybe I should separate her from Alex. He had been meeting her about once a week for coffee. She considered him a good shoulder to cry on. But the stories of the Frenchman were slowly driving Alex insane. Helen, I am sure, meant no harm. She was just so lost in her own heart that she couldn't see how obviously smitten with her Alex was. Now I suppose I could have Alex do a spell to attract Helen—but I don't know—the whole affair seemed so untidy.

It was at this point that I deposited the barely conscious Alex in a mild love healing and uncrossing bath. I then decided that I needed some help myself with this one. I immediately called a very powerful witch whom I consider my elder. Lady Lucinda has been around the block in love, and she knows all the spells for impossible situations. Luckily she was home and quite helpful with the information she revealed. According to Lady Lucinda, there was a very nasty spell done hundreds of centuries ago, and it has thrown the whole world off ever since. The spell was performed in ancient Greece by Paris. He wanted to win the love of Helen of Troy and steal her away from her husband, King Menelaus. While at sea, Paris shot down a sacred albatross. He spread the bird's huge wings across the eight-spoked wheel of his ship and then spun the helm around backward one full turn. By doing so, he caused Helen to believe she was madly in love with him. She subsequently left Menelaus to run off with Paris, thus causing the Trojan War. It is said that this spell was so powerful that it continues to throw off the mating pattern of the world. Everyone is one off. This, of course, would explain unrequited love as well as divorce. Those with weak Neptunian placements in their charts are still under this spell. Wow! I can always count on Lucinda to weave an enlightening tale. I felt chills run up and down my spine. Lucinda also said that each individual could reverse the spell by turning a ship's helm clockwise one full turn while calling out the names of all parties involved in the love triangle or quartet, as the case may be.

"Don't be puckish,* dear. It sounds like this poor fellow has already suffered enough mishaps in love. Don't try to enchant the girl for him until we find out the correct coupling of all parties involved." She then recommended this spell for Alex, saying that if indeed Helen were his soul mate, this reversal spell would set them right.

Now Lucinda is an old-fashioned witch and would never use supermarket ingredients. She said I absolutely must obtain an albatross with a minimum of an eight-foot wingspan and a ship's wheel with eight spokes. This is where Lucinda and I part ways. I left Alex soaking and went to the market, where I purchased a package of eight frozen turkey** wings. One down. On the way home I contemplated stealing someone's hubcap. What in the hell was I going to use for a wheel? Still racking my brain over this, I absentmindedly tripped over an open umbrella Alex had propped up in my hallway. It had been raining earlier in the evening when he arrived. I noticed the large bold letters and number embossed on the umbrella's side: *QE2*. Alex's last infatuation had been a nightclub singer on a ship. The *QE2,* to be exact. Alex had

*"Puck" is a nasty fairy who delights in wreaking havoc in love.
**Sacred Native American bird.

sailed around the world on the *Queen Elizabeth II* in pursuit of this woman. Unfortunately all he came home with was this big umbrella. Well, it's from a ship, I thought. That should do. No, wait, not only is it from a ship, it's an umbrella! Actually, any umbrella would do. A ship's helm navigates over the water, and an umbrella navigates through the water. In any case, both keep you from getting wet. "Witch's license. Witch's license," I sang in the hallway. I twirled the umbrella round and noticed it had eight spokes. Too good to be true. I snapped it shut and turned my key in the latch. Just then I heard the warning voice of my aunt Tabitha in my head: "You know better than to open an umbrella in the house, dear. It's bad luck." It was counterpointed by the voice of my spirit guide, Agnes Moorehead: "It's not bad luck if you open it upside-down. Then all the blessings will fall into it instead of falling out." I dismissed both of these voices, as I happen to know that the true origin of the umbrella superstition has to do with not wanting it to rain in your house. My ceiling had recently been recaulked, so there was no danger of leakage. Even so, I carefully opened the umbrella upside-down. I needed it that way anyway to be able to spin it round. I was waiting for the turkey wings to defrost when Alexander emerged from the bathtub. He was wearing my white silk robe and looked quite charming.

"Isn't that bad luck?" he remarked casually. "Don't you think I have enough of that already?"

I sat him down and explained all that had transpired. We stuck a thawed turkey wing through each of the umbrella spokes while I told the tale. Excited, color showing in his cheeks for the first time in months, Alex then rose to spin the wheel and chant:

> *Wheel of fortune, wheel of fate,*
> *This is Alex speaking.*
> *If Helen truly is my mate,*
> *Take her out of Manny's arms,*

Release her from the Frenchman's charms.
*Bring her home, bound to my soul where she belongs.**

He then spun the umbrella on its head with all his might. We both cried, overcome with emotion, and Alex claims he saw a vision as the turkey wings spiraled round. He said he saw himself and Helen in a past life quite similar to the way they had looked in all his dreams. They were kissing. He also saw Manny and the Frenchman dressed in armor, marching into a field of battle together. He had the impression they had been great generals and fought together. Well, it was quite an evening.

Nothing much happened for a while. But a year to the day after performing this spell, it seems they were all vacationing separately in France. Manny and the Frenchman unexpectedly ran into each other in front of the jewelry counter at Galeries Lafayette.** Apparently they were both purchasing a trinket for Helen. A fight ensued, both drew pistols, and each shot the other. Helen had been in the café, having a glass of wine. She arrived at the jewelry counter to find her husband and her lover lying dead in each other's arms. Helen was, of course, completely beside herself. A few moments later Alexander spotted her weeping over two dead bodies as he rode down the escalator. He had been on level three, buying lingerie for his beloved Helen. He rushed down and drew her to her feet. After a brief Q&A with the police, they exited Galeries Lafayette arm in arm. It was raining outside. Alex opened his huge *parapluie* to shelter them from the storm. They went out for a lovely pheasant dinner and never spoke a word—just gazed into each other's eyes. I understand they are now living somewhere on the Left Bank in quiet bliss.

*Please make up your own chant.
**French for Macy's.

PROMISED LAND

Ingredients:

    raisins
    almonds
    milk
    honey

This spell is to bring about a relationship with a soul mate, someone with whom you will feel a divine connection. All of these foods are mentioned in the Bible in association with the Promised Land. The Promised Land is often interpreted as coming home in a love relationship. Eat these foods to attract a holy relationship, one that is filled with God.

Raisins and almonds are said to make someone hear and recognize the call of home. In all my years of reading the tarot, the most commonly asked question is "Is he/she *the one?*" Raisins and almonds will help you answer this question for yourself.

Milk and honey are mixed to find happiness and bring fulfillment in love. Milk is also nurturing and represents fertility. For more information on honey, check the "Bees' Knees" section.

If you want to attract a soul mate, eat raisins and almonds with a glass of warm milk with a teaspoon of honey stirred in. If you want to know if someone specific is your soul mate, before retiring, drink a glass of warm milk with a teaspoon of honey stirred in. Place three raisins and three almonds under your pillow. Your dreams will reveal the answer to your question.

SEAN'S APPLE LOVE SPELL

Ingredients:

> **pink candles**
> **red apple**

This spell was given to me by a wonderful witch named Sean. It was given to him by his grandmother and is an old Spanish love spell. On the new moon take a pink candle, light it, and drip the wax onto a red apple. Do this for one minute and then extinguish the candle. Continue to drip wax on the apple every night until the moon is full. On the full moon, peel the pink wax drippings off the apple and bite into it. You will then find your one true love.

Pink is the color of sexual attraction, and red is the color of deep abiding love. Repeat this spell on the next new moon if no one *special* has entered your life by that time. General rule of thumb for those patient magicians is to have confidence in the first performance and wait up to one year (a complete lunar cycle) for your wish to be granted.

GOOD TOAD SPELLS FOR THE TWENTY-FIRST CENTURY

Dedicated to Bill Taylor

1. It is said that kissing (or eating) frogs' legs on a blue moon will attract your soul mate. A blue moon happens when there are two full moons in the same month. The second full moon is the blue one.

2. To turn a cheating lover into a toad. Ha. You wish!

3. Toads and frogs are actually sacred to the love goddess Venus as one aspect of the triple goddess Hecate. It is bad luck to kill them, just as it is considered bad luck to kill spiders or cats. Many ancient love spells use ingredients like dried toad. It is best to honor these creatures and live alongside them instead of dicing them up for a potion. Holding a frog, even having a frog cross your path, can bring fertility or prosperity into your relationship.

4. Based on Old English folk songs, it is believed that frogs can be of great luck to the courter. He or she need merely come in contact with or meditate upon the image of a frog, and he or she will be a master of the wooing arts.

5. Kissing a frog will not find you a Prince Charming, but it may find you a hopping good pet. However, if your pet frog falls asleep in your slipper while you are sweeping, you will marry a rich and charming man (but he will be a royal pain in the foot).

PET LOVE SPELL

Ingredients:

> **pet toy**
> **pet food**
> **white string**
> **red candle in a candle holder**

Among witches, it is common to perform rituals when a pet dies to insure that the soul of this pet will return to the witch as soon as possible. I have heard many amazing pet reincarnation stories. Things have happened to prove beyond a shadow of a doubt that the new black puppy, Hecate, is really the soul of that old orange puss, Pywacket. If you have lost an animal that is dear to you, perform this spell on the new moon (or on Halloween) to call your loved one home.

Take a favorite toy (it is okay to duplicate an old favorite that has been thrown out) or dish full of your pet's favorite food and tie a white string around the toy or the dish of cat or dog or bird or snake or fish or turtle or toad food. Tie the other end of the string around a candle holder. Anoint a red candle with a mixture of rosewater, lemon juice, and cinnamon extract. Place the candle in the holder and surround the candle holder with a circle of uncooked jasmine rice. These ingredients are used in a traditional witch's blend called Come to Me. Their combined energies create a very powerful attraction formula. You may also place a picture of your deceased pet on this altar. Pray to the goddess for the safe return of your pet as you gaze into the candle flame. When the candle has finished burning untie the white string from both ends and wrap it round the index and middle finger of your right hand. When you wrap the string be sure to move in circles toward your heart. This is a technique witches call cording to get someone to return home. Concentrate on your pet as you wrap the string round your fingers. After thirteen minutes cut the string from your fingers and imagine all obstacles being cut away from your pet returning to you. By the full moon begin to look for signs of the animal's return. Remember, he or she may not look quite the same. Nonetheless you will be able to recognize each other.

This spell can also be used to find a lost pet. Do all the above, except do not place a picture of the animal on the altar. Place something that belongs to them there instead. It is my belief that a picture of a living being should never be placed in front of a burning candle.

LONGEVITY AND PROTECTION

OK SPELL

Ingredients:

> orchid (or vanilla bean)
> kiwi fruit

A gentleman said to me after my first book came out, "Ha! If I can get her in the bath with the oranges and mint, then why do I even need a love spell?" Good question. Basic rule of thumb in love magic, as in anything else: Get them while they're young. I can't begin to count the number of men and women who have stopped coming to see me one to six months into a relationship, and then all of a sudden there they were, crying on the stoop of the shop, scrambling to make an appointment with me because things began to go wrong.

Start your love maintenance magic when all is well. Anticipate what the problems may be and start to work on them right away. OK comes from World War I, meaning *"zero (0) killed."* The OK Spell should be performed while both parties in the relationship are still *alive* and cooking. Don't wait until the passion has died. If you perform this spell twice a year on the new moons of both your signs, that should keep things running smoothly. If you are the same sign, do the spell twice a year, on the new and full moon in your joint sign (see "Moon Phases").

The orchid and the kiwi are both extremely delicate and perishable items. Yet one has a smell that lingers and the other a taste that lingers. You must approach your relationship as such. It is of a delicate nature, and you must learn how to preserve the preciousness within it. This is the spell to keep alive that magic that we always feel in the beginning stages of love.

In Mexico the orchid is a gift from the goddess to mortal lovers. It is meant to provide them with pleasure and happiness until their ultimate union with her. Vanilla beans are the fermented fruit of the vanilla orchid and can be used as a substitute for orchids in this spell. To the magician, the orchid represents the ultimate in mental powers and is used to focus the will. Orchid or vanilla bean preserves the intensity of a relationship and keeps the direction of your thoughts and feelings turned toward each other.

The kiwi is a fruit of love and passion. It is soft and vulnerable and can keep you from hardening toward each other. The kiwi also has another magical attribute. There is a bird in New Zealand called the kiwi. The kiwi is flightless and lives out its entire life with its feet planted firmly on the ground. The kiwi fruit will keep you grounded in your love and insure that you never fly from each other.

In the afternoon or morning on the appointed date, take two orchids (or vanilla beans) and two kiwi fruits and place one on your pillow and one on your partner's pillow. Leave them there all day. At night before you go to sleep, hold your orchid (or vanilla bean) under the nose of your partner for him/her to smell. Have your partner do the same for you. Peel the kiwi on your pillow and feed to your partner. Have him/her do the same for you. Kiss each other and state all the reasons why you love each other and want to remain together forever. Thank the goddess for all you have and ask her to continue blessing your relationship. You may then sleep, dream, or make love. You can even continue to talk. Do not, however, get up to work, watch TV, or turn on any lights until morning. You should remain in bed together until sunrise unless, of course, nature calls.

TREES OF LOVE

Ingredients:

   cherries
   chestnut
   pear
   maple
   fig
   apple

An old fairy love spell involved placing a written request for love inside a crevice of a tree of love. Another version of this spell was to carve the initials of the lovers upon the bark of a tree of love and encircle them with a heart to protect and lend longevity to the relationship. Traditional trees of love are cherry, chestnut, pear, maple, fig, and apple. A supermarket version of this ancient sorcery would be to carve your initials and your lover's initials into the fruit of any of these trees. Apples and pears are the easiest. Figs are a bit difficult if dry, wonderful and very powerful if fresh. The outer shell of the chestnut works well for scratching initials into, as it almost resembles the bark of a tree. As for cherries, a delicate operation, I suggest instead saving the stems of all you eat and then using them to form letters and a heart. If you want to invoke the love spirits of the maple tree, pour initials and a heart onto your pancakes with maple syrup.

Of course, all fruits of love should be ingested after carving. A chestnut can be saved and carried as a magical talisman.

SPELL TO KEEP A RELATIONSHIP FROM ENDING

Ingredients:

   root vegetables

Root vegetables are the best magical ingredient for giving *stick-to-it-iveness* to a relationship. Sometimes it is easier just to give up and move on instead of going deeper with your partner. This spell is most effective when worked while the relationship is still relatively happy and problem free. It will then create a great magical reserve of strength to be used when the relationship crosses over its abyss. If you begin working this spell when the relationship has already hit rock bottom, it will not produce the same reservoir of strength, but it can still be effective when used in conjunction with love healing spells.

   A potato is the easiest root vegetable to use for this spell. It is the catch-all of root vegetables and encourages nurturing and compassion. You can also use garlic, carrots, beets, or onions, although they may take longer to sprout. Use garlic if you need more passion and drive and if sexual problems are driving a wedge between you. Carrots are used for communication. Beets help overcome challenges and are used to keep the couple together for the long haul. Using an onion will help if there is anger between the couple. You can use all five vegetables as a wonderful maintenance spell to keep the relationship grounded in passion, communication, nurturing, understanding, and longevity. You can buy produce and keep it out until it begins to grow roots, although I usually find rooted vegetables lurking in the vegetable bin of my refrigerator every few weeks. Do not hesitate to use these lurkers for magical purposes. It is much better than just throwing them out. Once the vegetable has grown roots, follow these steps:

1. Hold the roots over a picture of yourself and your beloved. Rub the roots across the image.
2. Take the rooted vegetable and walk around the whole house with it, blessing and consecrating the space.
3. Keep them under your bed for a new-to-full-moon period (approximately two and a half weeks).
4. If possible, bury them around the outside of your house the day after the full moon. If this is not possible, bury them in the bottom of potted plants. If this is not possible either, then cut off the roots that have grown. Dispose of the rest of the vegetable. Add these root stocks to your mop water and wash down the house. For those with wall-to-wall carpeting, add the roots to a spray bottle filled with spring water and spray clockwise around the whole house.
5. Thank the roots and dispose of them properly. If you have buried them, this is considered a proper disposal. The second best method of disposal is to place them in a mulch. The third best way is to place them in the trash.

If you are doing this as a maintenance spell, three to four times a year should be sufficient. Some people like to repeat the spell at each change of season. For those in serious trouble, repeat every new moon until the relationship appears more stable.

SPELL TO PROTECT YOURSELF FROM AN ANGRY SPOUSE OR EX

Ingredients:

  salt
  vinegar
  potato

Salt purifies, vinegar drives away evil or danger, and potatoes are used for protection, comfort, and well-being. Of course, the quick version of this spell would be to eat salt-and-vinegar potato chips on the dark moon. If you need to work the spell on a more consistent basis and don't want to spoil your diet, make a protection bottle. Slice a white potato into quarters. This will protect you from all four quarters, or directions. Put the potato slices into an empty mayonnaise jar. Fill the jar almost to the top with vinegar. Add three tablespoons of salt. Shake this bottle whenever you feel threatened by your spouse or ex-spouse. This spell is based upon the Witch's Bottle. This bottle is made on the dark moon to ward off all danger.

LOVE AND PROTECTION SPELL

Dedicated to John Irving (the sexiest man alive) and his wife

Ingredients:

> **red radishes**
> **salt**
> **beer**

This spell is considered a maintenance spell. Nothing need be wrong in order for you to do it. It is designed to keep a relationship strong and healthy. If the relationship already has problems, you must use another spell first (see ''Love Healing Bath'') to remove the obstacles. Once the problems have cleared up, you may perform this spell. The one exception is if the problems are coming from an outside source (someone is jealous of your relationship or trying to meddle). In such cases, this spell works wonders in removing the evil and interfering eye.

Radishes, salt, and beer are all protective foods that keep negativity at bay. Radishes can also invoke hot and fiery love and passion. Eat salted radishes and drink beer with your lover on a new moon.

You can also let a radish grow roots, clip them off on a full moon, and place the radish roots in a jar filled with beer and three pinches of salt. Add to this a piece of paper with both parties' names written on it. (You may substitute hair clippings from both parties for written names.)

Close tightly and seal with wax drippings of both a red and a white candle. Hide the jar under your bed to protect the relationship.

SARAH'S SPELL FOR A WANDERING MATE

Ingredients:

> **stainless-steel tie-out stake**
> **assorted articles of unwashed clothing**

Sarah lives in Boston, and who can forget what they did to witches in the state of Massachusetts? Despite the enlightening strides achieved by Laurie Cabot, the official witch of Salem, some Massachusetts witches still feel threatened by the Puritan crowd. Sarah had two dilemmas. Not only were her neighbors nosy, but she also suspected that her husband, Cory, was cheating on her. Sarah wanted to work a very powerful spell to keep Cory at home. The problem was how to work it without the neighbors catching on.

She was afraid to go out in this neighborhood with her sword, lest someone see her and call the cops to have her arrested for attempted murder or, even worse, practicing satanic rites. Witches, by the way, use their swords or *athames* (daggers) to draw down power. It is a representation of the will and is never used to cut anything—vegetable, animal, mineral, or otherwise.

I happened to have been in town that week for a broomfest.

"Let's go shopping," I suggested.

While strolling down the pet aisle in the local Boston supermarket, I noticed this amazing magical item. I twirled it round and round in my hands, feeling its energy. I stretched out my hand and offered the object to Sarah.

"What is it?" she asked.

"It's your new sword," I exclaimed. I watched her eyes light up as her hand encircled the thing. There was no denying its power.

"It's intended to limit the movement of dogs, but I think it might be the perfect item for your wandering Cory." I smiled.

Sarah kept silent but continued to twirl my *wyrd** discovery round in her hands, musing.

"A lot of magic here," she finally conceded. She then turned the bright orange price sticker over and read: "Tie-out stake. $6.99. I can afford it."

The tie-out stake is made of stainless steel, just like the witch's dagger. Its hilt, or handle, is in the form of a triangle, representational of the triple goddess. From the hilt, the tie-out stake spirals down to a double-edged point. The witch's sword, or athame, must have a double-edged blade. In Sumerian temples the spiral represented the serpent guardians. Witches perform a sacred movement known as the spiral dance to penetrate the core of the goddess and her mysteries.

"I think *she* can be summoned through this tool," I whispered, placing my hand on top of Sarah's hand, which was wrapped tightly around the spiral.

The third sacred symbol was placed on the neck of the instrument, midway between the triangle hilt and the spiral. It was a ring or a circle. The circle represents the four directions. The magic circle is the place where witches raise energy.

Of course, the ring, or loop, is meant for attaching a leash. The spiral twists into the ground so that the dog cannot go far. The large triangle handle is probably designed to give one a good grip as one twists the tie-out stake into the ground.

Wyrd means "witch" or "goddess of fate." The *wyrdes* weave the destiny of man.

"We are women who see things beyond their ordinary nature," I said to Sarah. She leaned over and kissed me. I could feel the passion for magic rising in her.

"Let's go. I want to do a spell before the moon goes void of course."

She quickly purchased the stake and dragged me home with her. A full moon was going to occur that night at exactly midnight. At thirteen minutes after midnight the moon would go void of course.

At the witching hour, Sarah stepped out in the front yard. She held the tie-out stake up to the moon. I saw the moonbeams illuminate the triangle and travel down the spiral and into the double-edged point. Just then we heard some rustling in the bushes. The nosy neighbor Gladys* appeared between the azaleas.

"Just looking for the evening news," lied Gladys.

"Just checking for rain," lied Sarah, moving the tie-out stake behind her back.

"Well, good night, then," said Gladys while giving me a curious once-over.

"Night," said Sarah between her teeth.

Sarah and I are actually old pointed hats when it comes to dealing with inquisitors. You see, we were both burned at the stake together in a past life. Not in Salem, but Germany. During the Middle Ages. When we met again in this life, we vowed to protect each other and to never let anyone stand in the way of the work of the goddess.

"I have an idea," I whispered, and I led Sarah toward the two-car garage. We entered and closed the doors behind us. The garage had a small skylight that no one could see through. However, the light of the moon shone directly through it. Sarah stood underneath these sacred rays and slowly lifted her dress. She carefully placed the stake against her body and shivered a bit from the cold. She motioned for me to come to her. I must say that it is moments such as these that remind me how much I love being a priestess and witch. I began unbuttoning my shirt and moved toward her until I too stood in the light of the luminous moon. I pressed my chest to hers so that we held the tie-out stake between our breasts. I wrapped my arms around her, she wrapped her arms around me, we uttered the sacred names of the god and goddess,

---

*Name changed to reflect the nature of the guilty party.

and we hugged each other for all we were worth. When witches consecrate a sacred tool, such as a sword or dagger, they place it (point down) between the hearts of two witches and charge it with love and power. I closed my eyes and pressed my lips against Sarah's lips. We sealed the consecration with a kiss.

"Oh, my goddess! I only have five minutes," she cried, and dashed through the adjoining garage door into the house. I followed her into the laundry room while buttoning up my shirt.

She rummaged through some dirty laundry, held up a pair of men's underwear, and shouted: "This is it!"

I will not go into the myriad thoughts that crossed my mind at that moment.

"No, it's not," said Sarah, flinging the Fruit of the Loom briefs in my general direction. "This is it!" she exclaimed, brandishing one of Cory's dirty socks. She quickly tied it in a knot around the loop of the tie-out stake. My mind swiftly recovered from its naughty interlude, and I began to catch on. The circle represents what you want to protect or hold on to. This is where you will tie the article of clothing that serves as a stand-in for your lover. It is best to use unlaundered garments, as they hold the sweat or scent needed to form the sympathetic magical link. Using a sock will literally bring his or her feet back through the door. Underwear will bring him/her back sexually. Neckties and bras summon the return of the heart and throat (communication).

Sarah ran back into the front yard and twisted the tie-out stake into the ground while whispering these words:

By the power of Circle, Spiral, and Triple mother
Bind Cory to me, keep him away from any other.

I heard another rustling in the azaleas, and I looked at my watch. Thirteen minutes after midnight. Perfect timing. Gladys once again emerged from the bushes.

"Whatcha doing?" she asked.

"Setting up my tie-out stake," answered Sarah as she rose and dusted off her hands.

"But you don't own a dog," Gladys stated emphatically.

"Well, I'm thinking of getting one. A large one, to keep pests out of my azaleas," retorted Sarah.

"Oh my!" was the reply as Gladys scurried back into her house. Sarah and I went inside and had a cup of tea and some cakes. About fifteen minutes had passed when we heard Cory's car pull into the driveway.

"He usually doesn't get home until three or four in the morning," said Sarah.

"The spell must be working," we both said, and laughed.

Cory walked into the kitchen and began apologizing. "I know you must be thinking that I'm up to no good. But I'm not, really. Tonight I just had this weird sense that I might be losing you, so I decided to put all my work aside. In fact, I'm taking some time off, so for the next two weeks, I'm completely yours."

I took that as my cue to exit. Sometimes a witch's work is truly done. As I drove through the Boston streets, I marveled at the essential beauty of supermarket sorcery. You no longer have to thrust Excalibur through your driveway to get your husband to come home. These days all you need is a tie-out stake on the front lawn. The modern-day inquisitor will have difficulty in declaring you a witch, even if you don't happen to own a dog.

LOVE OUANGA

Ingredients:

> **two kitchen magnets**
> **ginger powder**
> **orange peel**
> **cardamom seeds**
> **rose petals**
> **uncooked rice**

sugar
matches
cheesecloth bag or small plastic bag
red twist tie or red rubber band or red shoelace

A ouanga bag is a witch's magical bag (usually made of silk cloth) into which special herbs have been stuffed to create a specific magical effect. Ouangas can be made for health, wealth, success, or love. This recipe is a modified version of a love ouanga from a witch's *grimoire* (book of recipes).

The first step is to find two kitchen magnets that will attract. The magnets will represent the couple. Traditional witches use a special rock called a lodestone, which has magnetic properties. Drop the magnets into the bag. Sprinkle ginger on top to insure that the spice and magnetism remain. Orange peel is for love and commitment, cardamom for eroticism, and rose petals for friendship. Add rice to give the relationship strength and longevity. The custom of throwing rice at newlyweds stems from China, where the belief is that eating rice out of a common bowl will bind the souls together. Sprinkle sugar (a teaspoon) to sweeten the life you will share.

It is also traditional to take a hair clipping from each party, braid them together, and add it to the bag. If you are doing this spell to attract a new and unknown lover, do not worry about the hair. Do not add your own hair, either. Instead sprinkle cinnamon (a teaspoon) in the bag to create drawing power.

Shake the bag and state or think or visualize all that you wish for this union. The bag is now ready to be activated. It must be charged with the four elements: earth, air, fire, and water. The herbs already constitute the earth element. Strike a match and throw it in the bag to include the fire element. Quickly (and I mean quickly) blow out the match in the bag. Your breath is the air element. Spit in the bag to add the water element. Saliva (along with other bodily fluids) was considered very powerful and sacred by the ancient alchemists. Your breath and saliva also add a personalized touch to the spell. They are in essence a magical Social Security number so that there is no mistaken identity. Remember, the gods get a lot of requests (and I mean a lot!).

You want to make sure you have the correct return address on your spell. The last remaining task is to tie the bag with a red twist tie or rubber band or shoelace. Use red or pink, as they are the colors of love. You may keep the ouanga bag on your altar, on top of a picture of you and your love. You may stuff it under a pillow or bed. The most common use of a ouanga is to carry it near the heart, in a breast pocket or a brassiere.

SPELL TO PREVENT STDs

Ingredients:

> **lavender**
> **thyme**
> **heather flowers or heather soap (can substitute sage)**
> **balsamic vinegar**
> **bergamot (an Earl Grey teabag)**

All of these herbs combined are considered herbs of protection and house or temple blessing. The body is a house or a temple, and we must respect it as such. Lavender relaxes the body, alleviating stress, and combined with thyme, it becomes a strong protection formula. Heather (or sage) can actually tone down the sex drive. Balsamic vinegar has a very sobering effect on the brain. Bergamot is sacred to San Juan Conquistador (High John the Conqueror). Many occult practitioners summon this saint for health and wise counsel. He is known to lead one away from all danger.

This spell cannot protect you while you are having sex (protected or unprotected), but it can help you relax, stop to assess the situation, and think your way through it, instead of doing something risky without giving it much thought until the fretting of the morning after.

Obtain a small bottle with a tight-fitting lid and fill it with five tablespoons of balsamic vinegar, three pinches each of lavender and thyme, three heather flowers or three shavings from a heather soap bar (or three pinches of sage). Open an Earl Grey teabag and pour the contents into the jar. Earl Grey contains bergamot oil, and black tea is used to divine the future.

Carry this small bottle with you, and if you find yourself about to enter into a sexual situation, simply open and run the bottle under the nose. Inhaling the scent should protect you and help you to make the right decision. Maybe the decision is to wait, maybe it's to go ahead, or maybe it is to say no. Trust your instincts. Please take the time to breathe and assess. You are worth it.

Note: This spell is in no way, shape, or form to replace safer sex methods. It is designed only to help you think before you act.

Triple XXX Hexes and Xtra Added Love

XXX FOR KISSES

In early Christian times, the X was used for a signature. People would also kiss the X in the same way they kissed a Bible to take an oath or show their allegiance. Eventually the X's came to symbolize love or kisses when signing off a letter. Take a blank piece of red or white paper and draw three large X's in the center. You are going to create a magical talisman for love.

When you draw the three X's, connect the points of the middle X to the points of the X's on the right and on the left of it. You should now have a glyph that looks like an M crossed over a W—or, as I like to think, an upright and an upside-down W, for double Witch Power. This symbol is actually part of the witch's alphabet, and it symbolizes the perfect union. You will notice there are now two diamond shapes in the center of the glyph. As they say, diamonds are forever. Write your name in one diamond and write the name of the one you love in the other diamond. Leave this talisman upon your altar to charge. You may also carry it with you near your heart.

The X is the letter of the four directions. Writing your names within the X's will give you protection from all four quarters. In the runic alphabet, X is known as *gifu.*

The rune of *gifu* means gift and partnership. To let your partner know what a gift you consider him or her, cross your thumbs to make an X and press them against your partner's lips. Kiss your partner over your thumbs three times. The thumb is the digit of Venus. Sometimes the simplest spell will have the most powerful effects. Perform on a full moon to keep the magic alive in your relationship.

HEX YOUR EX

Ingredients:

> **figs**
> **cucumbers**

For those of you who want a "get even" spell, this would be the one. Of course, the higher road would be the Love Healing Bath. But some of us travel the low road. One of the most useful purposes of this spell is the cleansing and cathartic experience afforded the practitioner. Whether or not the spell actually affects the ex-lover is not as important as the anger it releases from within the practitioner. Usually the spell will mildly affect the party on whom it is performed and greatly improve the emotional and spiritual state of the one who is performing it. However, the more often the spell is repeated, the more negative will be the effect it will have upon both parties. The ex will become blocked in love and sexual fulfillment, while the practitioner may become melancholic and more and more obsessive. It is best to perform this spell only once and then be done with it.

Figs were sacred in matriarchal societies because they represented the female genitals. In medieval times they were shunned by church fathers as licentious and evil fruit. Some even believe it was a fig and not an apple that Eve tempted Adam with. The fig has been firmly established throughout time as a surrogate for the vagina. Cucumbers (or zucchini, if you will) are a common modern representation or surrogate for the male genitals. To work this spell, choose the fruit or vegetable that is representative of the sex of your former partner. Carve his or her name into the cucumber or fig as you visualize his or her genitals. Place the fig or cucumber into the freezer. This should be done on a waning moon. The effects of this spell will be to freeze the genitals of your partner, thereby preventing him or her from experiencing any sexual pleasure. This spell seems to work best when the former partner was known to be cheating on you during the course of the relationship. It can also be performed on two parties if you know whom your partner left you for. In such a case, the practitioner—let's call her Sonja, a beautiful European socialite—would use one zucchini labeled "Ronald" for her land-grubbing, skirt-chasing ex-husband and one fig carved with the name "Georgia" for the big blond bimbo Ronnie left her for. The spell can also be worked on a current partner who you are sure is having an affair. Do not perform this on a current partner unless you are completely sure he or she is cheating. Otherwise he/she will lose all interest in having sex with you and will probably go out and have an affair.

Remove the frozen items after thirteen days and bury them in the ground. This last part of the ritual is designed for the practitioner. It will not harm the ex-lover. The burial serves as a ritual to help you to completely let go of your no-good ex. Even if you still want him or her back, remember the old adage "Plant you now, dig you later." Now is the time to let it go. Follow up with Masha's Mourning Spell if necessary.

HEX YOUR BED SPELL

Ingredients:

> **mustard seed**
> **cardamom**
> **marjoram**

If your bed is the place that inspires your lover to nod off to sleep, you need this spell. Lift up the mattress and sprinkle these spices clockwise in a circle. Chant the following:

> *Enchant Bewitch my Bed*
> *Create passion from toe to head*
> *may [add name]*
> *be struck with desire for me*
> *while in this bed so mote it be.*

Mustard is the great awakener. The hotter, the spicier, the sexier, mustard provokes the imagination and can make one more creative. Marjoram is a love spice that also stimulates talk. Communication in bed is a very important element to a good relationship. Cardamom is a dreamy aphrodisiac; if put under the bed, it can make you wake up in the mood.

ELIXIR OF BLISS

Ingredients:

  jasmine rice
  orange flower water
  rosewater
  sweet coconut milk (canned)
  white cardamom seeds
  pinch of curry

This blend summons scenes from the *Kama Sutra* and works on two fronts. First, it influences the olfactory senses; and second, it acts as an edible love potion. You can prepare this on your own as a spell to attract a blissful relationship or even a blissful evening within a miserable relationship. You can also use it with a partner to prolong a state of bliss. Cooking this blend while making love can prolong both male and female orgasm. Eating it afterward can renew desire for more lovemaking and prolong the euphoric state of love. *Caution: Do not prepare this elixir if you have to drive or operate heavy machinery immediately afterward.*

Add one and a quarter cups of water to a saucepan. Add half a cup of sweetened coconut milk. Add one-eighth cup of rosewater and one-eighth cup of orange flower water. Bring to a boil. Shell five white cardamom seeds and crush seeds in mortar and pestle. Add to water. Add one cup jasmine rice. Cover and reduce heat. Let cook for thirty minutes. The aroma that will fill the room is the supermarket equivalent of ancient tantric incense from the Levant. It will arouse the passions and stir the souls to love. After the brew is done, let sit for seven minutes, then stir and serve. Eating this mixture is said to return one to the state of original paradise. It is alleged to remove all feelings of sin and guilt surrounding sexual love.

Rose, jasmine, and orange are all flowers of love. Cardamom is a lustful herb that when held under the tongue is said to bring one to a state of rapture. The Chinese traditionally use rice to unite the souls of lovers on their wedding night. We continue this custom today by throwing rice at newlyweds. Coconut is used to summon purity in love and to remove any and all harmful and unwanted influences. You may add a pinch of curry if you need a bit more heat in your relationship. I don't mean warmth, I mean heat. Use curry if cuddling has replaced coupling.

SPELL TO WIN BACK AN EX LOVE

Ingredients:

> **a purple potato**
> **dark chocolate morsels**
> **a knife**

Create a Mr. or Mrs. or Ms. Potato Head with a knife and a purple potato.* We use purple because it is the color of power. Place a hair clipping of your ex on top of the head to create the magical link. This is known as poppet magic and is a very powerful way to influence someone. Witches design poppets out of cloth, but in Neolithic times potatoes were used as poppets. The poppet is then stuffed with the appropriate herbs for healing, love, revenge, and so on to create the desired effect upon the subject.

Carve a hole in the back of the potato head and fill it with chocolate morsels. Then carve your name deeply across the forehead. Whenever your name comes to mind, your ex will experience the endorphin rush that chocolate brings. Feelings of love for you will once again manifest. You can also use a second potato and carve a heart on its surface. Fill the heart with chocolate morsels as well to reopen his or her heart to you. Keep the poppet under your pillow or on your love altar until this person returns to you.

*Purple potatoes can be found in organic produce markets. If you cannot obtain a purple potato, you may substitute red.

XANADU

Ingredients:

wishbone from a turkey or chicken
knotted pretzel

Xanadu oil is a special wishing oil used to bless a couple with prosperity and make their dreams come true. The ingredients of this oil are a closely guarded secret, but all of them have one property in common: they are alleged to make wishes come true. The supermarket equivalent to Xanadu oil would be wishbones and knotted pretzels. The ancient custom of pulling a wishbone and making a wish is also done in Switzerland with the knotted pretzel. It is traditional for a married couple to make a wish over a knotted pretzel on their wedding day.

Make a ouanga bag for you and your mate with a turkey wishbone and a knotted pretzel. Rub the ouanga bag whenever you need to make a wish for the relationship. You can also pull a wishbone or knotted pretzel with your mate and make a common wish as you do so. No one ends up with the short end in this ritual. The breaking of the bone or pretzel is a magical act of release that will make your wish manifest. In fact, it is customary to call out the wish jointly as you break the bone or pretzel between you.

XAVIER'S SPELL

Ingredients:

all hard-shelled nuts

Xavier had a problem with the ladies. He also had a problem with pornography. Xavier could never get a date, so he spent all his time going to the triple-X-rated peep shows. Xavier's aura was full of *kooties*. No one wanted to come near him, especially me. The first time he appeared at the shop, we let our Klingon warrior handle Xavier. The Klingon warrior handles all of our most difficult cases. Klingon smudged him with sage and immediately took some of that nasty gunk out of his auric field. Xavier actually started to look like a normal guy. He still had a problem with the ladies, though. You see, Xavier was so hard up, he was much too much of an eager beaver in love.

"Xavier," I said to him after listening to the umpteenth story of his sad and disgusting attempts to score, "never ask a lady to go home with you after a few whirls around the dance floor. *Très gauche.* How eighties of you! Get with it, son. Modern romance takes patience and cultivation. You act like some kind of crazed nut."

Xavier nodded his head wildly in agreement.

What a nut, I thought. *Nut.* Of course, Xavier needs the nut spell to slow him down. When a person is imbalanced in his or her sexuality, it is wise to use nut magic. Nuts are brain food,* to crack them takes patience, and their shells** can be used to either increase or decrease the sexual drive. Xavier needed a major decrease. The removal of nuts from their shells could help him accomplish that. I told him to go home, throw out all his "too disgusting to even divulge the nature of" videotapes and girly mags, and crack 1,020 nuts slowly on the dark moon.

"What kinds of nuts?" he asked lecherously.

"All kinds, every kind, I don't care what kind, any kind you can get your hands on, just keep your hands off your own!" I bellowed. "And don't eat any of those nuts until they've all been cracked," I added.

He nodded insanely.

"Then take each and every nutshell half and turn them down like little inverted

---

*Except for almonds and pistachios, which put your head right back in your pants.
**See "Incubus and Succubus Spell" for more about shells.

bowls. Spread them round in a large circle about the floor. Stand in the center of that circle and gather all the nut flesh and pound it to a pulp by hand with a mortar and pestle. Surround yourself in a second smaller circle of powdered nuts and pray for patience, penance, purity, and peanuts. Do not leave this circle for twelve hours,'' I commanded.

Xavier promised to comply. I sent Klingon along home with him to collect all the smut. Honestly, I couldn't think of anything from the supermarket that could coerce this guy into changing his rating from triple X to PG. I can only perform that kind of magic with the help of my trusty assistant Joey, known by all as the Klingon warrior. When Joey asks you to do him a favor, you do it. Like magic. One look into those beastly red eyes, one glimpse of those large silver-ringed knuckles heading toward your beautiful face, and like I said, you do it. Whatever Joey wants, you do it. Like magic.

Now I am in no way advocating violence, but let me just say that this guy Xavier has been in a Twelve Step program for sex addicts for thirteen years. It hasn't done him much good. Desperate cases call for desperate measures. I will say, in defense of the goddess, that cracking all those nuts did do him a lot of good. He has been on his best behavior, his aura is squeaky clean, and he's taken three women out on four coffee dates each.

On the first date, they had Hawaiian macadamia coffee and talked about what wonderful weather we've been enjoying. A miracle! Got past the first date without scaring them off or turning them off. On the southern pecan coffee date I understand he was a perfect gentleman. The third date was hazelnut coffee, where he discussed Einstein's theory of relativity. The last date, they ordered chocolate almond coffee, and I understand all three women ended their dates in exactly the same way—by slapping him across the face. Well, for Xavier, that's progress indeed!

By the way, Joey was happier than a pig in a starship on the last full moon. His bonfire blazed brighter than ever thanks to all the Xciting kindling, compliments of Xavier.

LOVE AND THE LAW

A WALK DOWN THE AISLE SPELL

Ingredients:

> **one whole chicken**
> **paprika**
> **fresh sage**
> **fresh rosemary**
> **tobacco**
> **white candles and paper doilies (optional)**

It was on a dark moon Friday, when I popped into the local supermarket to pick up a box of white candles and some paper doilies, that I first met Pauline. She was working the "under ten items" register. There was a long line and customers were complaining. Pauline was crying and shortly another cashier opened her booth. Everyone scrambled to be the first in the new checkout line, but I stayed behind, holding my white candles and doilies, to ponder Pauline's predicament.

Why would a woman working the under ten line cry? I would cry were I assigned to the regular register and had to ring up the people with two baskets full of groceries all day. At least hers was a fast-paced job.

"What's wrong, dear?" I asked.

Pauline was sniveling so much, she could barely talk. I suggested she take a break and stroll down the aisles with me. As we pushed a cart together, Pauline revealed to me the source of her woe. It seemed she had no green card and was forced to work this job off the books. In Hungary she had studied gynecological medicine, but she could not practice here until she got her citizenship. Pauline's scoundrel of a boyfriend had chicken feet and refused to marry her.

"You're in luck, Pauline, as I am a doctor of love." I laughed as we passed the fresh meat and poultry section. "Grab a chicken, please," I instructed her.

"Listen, if you give me a breast exam, I'll get you married. I'm just joking, Pauline!" I said while inspecting the bird she had placed in my hand. "Now tell me, what is considered the sexiest spice in your part of the world?"

"I don't know," she answered blankly.

"Oh, come on. Hungarians are poets, lovers, great cooks—of course you know," I cajoled.

"Paprika," she announced, her eyes lighting up. "My grandmother always said: 'A pinch of paprika to get a man, a pound of chicken to keep him.' Yes, that's just the way she put it."

"There you go, Pauline. You barely need my help with this one. I think, though, it would be good to add a little legal success to your love spell." I zoomed across to the produce section and pulled a bunch of fresh sage and rosemary to add to the cart. "Sage, rosemary, and tobacco are a common witch's blend for winning legal battles. So just remember to smoke a cigarette while you season your paprika chicken, Pauline."

She gave me a concerned look and arched her brow.

"One cigarette won't kill you," I insisted, and I handed her the white candles and paper doilies. "It never hurts to set a nice table, either. Good luck, dear."

I left the market empty-handed but feeling completely satisfied.

Pauline is now happily married and one of the top gynecologists in New York City. She also runs a free clinic for uninsured grocery checkout girls. I see her once a year for a Pap smear and every other month for a home-cooked Hungarian meal.

SPELL FOR PRENUPTIAL AGREEMENT

Ingredients:

> **clove**
> **rice**
> **dried lemon and lime and orange peel**
> **zipper-lock bag**

Clove and lime are used for influence, power, and protection of goods. Lemon is a purifying agent. Orange and rice are used to bless a union of love. The combination of all these ingredients will help you to agree upon some difficult legal terms without letting love fly out the window. If you need to protect your interests before getting married, make a ouanga bag with twenty cloves; the dried peels of one whole lime, lemon, and orange; and a fistful of uncooked rice. Place a copy of the prenuptial agreement in the bag, too. Add a lighted match, blow it out quickly, and then spit in the bag. Place the ouanga underneath the sofa when you sit down to discuss terms with your marriage-partner-to-be. Rest assured that all will go well.

SPELL FOR A GOOD DIVORCE ATTORNEY

Ingredients:

> **cinnamon**
> **lavender**
> **orange and purple candles**

Cinnamon is ruled by Mercury. Mercury is the ruler of communication. He is also the patron saint of tricksters, thieves, and lawyers. Orange candles are for success.

Rub cinnamon powder on orange candles when you want to attract a sharp talker who can win.

Lavender is sacred to Hermes. Purple is the color of wisdom. You want your representative to know the law. Purple is also used for power and influence and to win at court. Buy a lavender-scented purple candle or rub a purple candle with lavender oil or lavender flowers.

If you have already chosen a lawyer, carve his or her name along with your own on both candles to invoke legal success. Burn on a full moon. If you are looking for an attorney, burn the candles on a new moon. When they have finished burning, roll both candle drippings into one ball of wax. Carry this into court as a talisman for success. Or carry on interviews to help you choose the right representation.

SPELL FOR A GOOD DIVORCE SETTLEMENT

Ingredients:

> **cinnamon**
> **allspice**
> **tobacco**
> **sage**
> **bayberry**
> **green and purple candles**

This spell should be done on a full moon. Carve your name and your lawyer's name on a purple candle. Carve your name and the amount of money (or properties) you wish to secure from your settlement on a green candle. Do not put your lawyer's name on the green candle, as you will end up having nothing left after paying his/her fees! The green candle should be bayberry scented. The purple candle should be unscented or lavender scented only. If you cannot obtain a bayberry candle, use a stalk of bayberries. (They are usually available around Christmastime, so you might want to stash some away in case you ever decide to get divorced.) Surround these candles with a hefty circle of cinnamon powder, sage powder, allspice powder, and loose tobacco (and possibly bayberries). These ingredients are used by witches for money and legal success. Light the candles and let them burn completely. Roll up all the remains and mold into one big ball. Carry into court as a success talisman. This talisman should never be seen by anyone in the courtroom. It must remain hidden from view. The only exception is if a jury is involved. You can influence a jury by subtly letting them sneak a peek at your talisman.

SPELL TO PROTECT YOUR ASSETS DURING A DIVORCE

Ingredients:

**head of romaine lettuce
a silver coin**

Take a head of romaine lettuce and hold it up to your own head. Form a mental bond with the lettuce. As you insert a silver coin into its center, visualize your money being hidden from your former spouse and his/her attorneys. Visualize a certain sum or source of money being kept secret within your mind.

On the dark moon bury the head of romaine lettuce with the silver coin hidden inside. Surround the burial site of the romaine with a circle of white light (visualize this). Leave the place and do not look behind you. This will insure the safety of your assets.

This spell is based on the combination of two magical principles. The first stems from ancient Rome, where it was customary to hide coins in cabbage or lettuce heads to invoke prosperity. Romaine lettuce is best, as the leaves are dark green (more prosperous) and the crevices between the leaves are deeper than your ordinary iceberg.

Romaine lettuce is ideal to conceal, which leads to the second custom of burying treasure to hide and protect it. The earth is believed to be the goddess. All that we turn over to the soil will be guarded by her. You may also want to write the words ''private eye'' on a piece of paper and stick it in an ice-cube tray filled with water. Put the ice tray into the freezer. This will prevent any dick your ex may have hired from discovering your wealth.

Love, Melancholia, Mad Crushes, Fixations, Obsessive Behavior, and Borderline Stalking

What can I say? The majority of people who want a love spell fall into these categories. Poor babies. They have all been smitten themselves. Fallen prey to the sting of the love bug, they become mind-feverish, unable to hold a thought beyond that of the desired one. They live in a state of constant agitation. Having nowhere to turn for relief, they set out to enchant the object of their affections and seek to produce the same state of agitation in the desired one.

Listen to Lady Venus when she tells you that this is not nice. It is unkind. It is not an act of love. It is, however, an act of human nature. Reminds me of a Talmudic commentary written on the biblical story of Noah and the Flood. Apparently, when the deluge came, a band of drowning people tried to destroy Noah's Ark. It never even occurred to them to try to climb on board; they decided that if they were doomed to drown, they would take Noah and his lot down with them. What follows are some spells to save yourself from drowning in love. Before you attempt to pierce the heart of another, take a beat to calm and center your own heart. Make sure that what you desire is really for your highest good and for the highest good of another. Also included are spells to protect yourselves from the mad stalkers and remedies for melancholy babies.

COCONUT LOVE BREAKER

Ingredients:

one coconut

This spell is designed to relieve an aggravating obsession, the kind of love/hate that gives you a migraine. The coconut love breaker is the aspirin of the magical world. Severe agitation may be symptomatic of someone working magic on you against your will. You will know this to be so if you find yourself obsessing over a person or "falling in love" with someone whom you do not even particularly like.

Coconuts are sacred in the Caribbean and have long been used for cleansing and to break (as well as bind) love spells. If someone has cast a love spell on you, the spell can be broken by kicking a coconut across the floor and breaking it open as you do so. If the coconut does not break when you kick it, try again and again and again. The spell will not break until the coconut breaks. Try kicking it against a hard door or kick it outside against a cement wall. Also make sure the outer husk of the coconut has already been removed. You will be using the hard, ball-shaped center of the coconut for this spell. If you know the name of the person who has bewitched you, call it out as you kick, followed by the words:

Break! Brake! Stop! Now!
To your will I shall never bow
Break! Brake! Stop! Now!

If you do not know who the person is (but you feel vexed nonetheless), simply repeat the verse sans a name.

COCONUT HEAD WASH

Ingredients:

one whole coconut
a screwdriver
a hammer

This spell is used to alleviate obsessive thinking. Only you can determine what the safe amount of cerebral intake about your heart's desire is.

"Safe amount?" you say. "How could I possibly spend too much time thinking about him/her?"

How about when you spend ten hours of your employer's time composing a love letter to e-mail to your obsession? Or perhaps while driving that bus full of school-children, you run a red light because you are too distracted reliving the sense memories of the night before? Yes, my friend, it is time for a magic spell to put you on a mental diet.

Don't worry, this is relatively painless. Take a whole coconut and pry off the outer husk. It will be difficult, just as difficult as removing the object of your obsession from your mind. We will use a bit of sympathetic magic here. Visualize the coconut as your brain and you are in the process of stripping it bare. Once you reveal the hard ball shape within, roll it around your head in a counterclockwise motion. Move your head counterclockwise as well. Hold the coconut above your head and shake it. Hold it to the right, to the left, in front of your face, and finally behind your head. Each time you shake the coconut, shake your head. Shake loose the obsessive thoughts.

Now take a screwdriver and a hammer. (Here comes some delicate brain surgery.)

Place the point of the screwdriver on the dark indentations, or "nipples," of the coconut. Tap the handle of the screwdriver with the hammer to open the holes in the coconut (you can also use a drill for this procedure). Pour out the coconut milk into a glass or bowl. Then pour the milk over your head and rub your face and scalp very vigorously. The milk will cleanse and soothe your brain and spirit. Next, break the coconut all the way open. Take the larger half of the shell and carve into the coconut meat, using the screwdriver or drill bit* as a pen. Choose three to ten subjects of thought that you would like to replace the old obsessive thoughts. Here are some examples:

Instead of thinking about _____, I would like to focus on

1. what I'm really getting paid to do at my job.
2. traffic laws.
3. writing that screenplay.
4. a new and different cute person to obsess over.

After you have finished carving your new thoughts, place the coconut half over your head as if it were a thinking cap. Spend at least ten to twenty minutes in silent meditation. Do not—I repeat, *do not*—allow your thoughts to light upon you know who during this part of the ritual. If you need more self-control, take a slice of lime, anoint it with three drops of hot sauce, and place it under your tongue. You must use the thinking cap and do this meditation for seven days in a row. Afterward you must thank the coconut and dispose of it properly.

In such cases where you have been hurt by this person in your head and would choose never to think of him/her ever, ever again (which is quite different from someone you never, ever want to stop thinking about), the spell must be worked as follows. Begin the spell in the same fashion. Before carving new ideas into the larger half of the coconut, you will first take the smaller half and carve that person's name

*Detach from drill first, please!

into it. Bury the smaller half outdoors and then continue to carve the replacement thoughts into the larger half of the coconut. Follow spell to conclusion.

MASHA'S MOURNING SPELL

Medvedenko: Why do you always wear black?
Masha: I am in mourning for my life.

—The Seagull, *Anton Chekhov*

Ingredients:

**amphitheater (if possible); if not obtainable, use a private bathroom
    with a good echo and a nice porcelain edge on the tub
rolled-up newspaper (make sure it's yesterdays news)
black garment or a black dish towel pinned to your clothes
an artichoke
burdock root or parsnip**

This spell is designed for those who gravitate toward the dramatic. Ritual magic was practiced in the great Greek amphitheaters. Magic and drama have always been closely linked. An amphitheater is the best place for dramatic release. Mourning the loss of a relationship, the death of life as you knew it, is extremely important. Without taking the time to mourn, you cannot truly move on. It does not matter how the relationship died. A figurative death can be just as traumatic as a literal one.

Black is a sexy, moody, powerful, artistic, and temperamental color. Black is also the color of loss and mourning. In advanced magic, black is a color for healing and removing negative energy. You can wear black for seductive reasons. You can wear black to help heal yourself from a relationship that has ended. I recommend wearing black clothing for seduction, mourning, or power.

Act I. Stand in the middle of the amphitheater while wearing black. Throw your arms above your head and shout: "I just made up my mind that I would tear this love out of my heart, tear it out by the roots." If Chekhov's chant is not good enough for you, then make up your own:

"Hortense, stop taking up free rent in my head. I sincerely wish you were dead!"

"Good riddance, Gertrude," is good, or, "Good-bye forever, Godfrey."

Don't think about it too much, just shout out whatever comes off the top of your head. If an amphitheater is not available, go into the bathroom with a rolled-up newspaper and shout the name of your (for all intents and purposes) deceased lover as you whack the paper against the side of the tub. This is the time to be dramatic. Cry, scream, kick, and wail. Let yourself go. At this point you will rip the black garment or black dish towel that is pinned to your clothing.* The rending of clothing has been a rite of passage for mourners dating back to ancient times. It is still practiced by those of the Jewish faith.

Act II. The first act of this ritual was to put you in touch with your anger and to help release it. The second act is to put you in touch with your sorrow at losing all the wonderful parts of your mate that you sincerely love and will miss. Softly call out the name of your lost lover as you peel each and every leaf away from an artichoke until you reach the heart. The artichoke teaches us to examine our core and all the hard and soft feelings that surround it. Hold the heart of the artichoke next to your own and sit still for several minutes.

Act III. Remove all your clothing and run the bathwater. Add nine pieces of burdock root or parsnip. Nine is the number of endings and completion. Burdock and parsnip draw out bitterness and hopelessness from the heart. They are cleansing agents. Climb in the tub and soak for at least twenty minutes. Meditate upon closure and see yourself having everything you need (spiritually, emotionally, mentally, and physically) to move on.

---

*It is helpful beforehand to make a small incision in the garment with a scissors. That way it will be easy to tear.

This spell should be performed nine days before the new moon. Continue wearing black for empowerment until the new moon. On the new moon wear white for new beginnings.

THE GLOVE CLEANER

Ingredients:

> **yellow rubber gloves**
> **twelve sunflower seeds**
> **hydrogen peroxide**
> **sea salt**
> **blue or gray candle**
> **assorted other ingredients**

Remember the *Twilight Zone* episode of the same title? A man bought a love potion for one dollar. It worked quite well—in fact, too well. The adoring woman followed him around like a lovesick puppy. When he returned to buy the antidote, it cost one thousand dollars. The message here is that love spells are a dime a dozen; it's the spell to remove an annoying doter that is rare. The glove cleaner was actually poison fed to the lover, as the only way to break the spell was to kill her.

My glove cleaner spell is much more cost-effective and not in the least bit deadly. You will need a pair of yellow rubber gloves and twelve sunflower seeds. Obtain a mortar and pestle and grind each sunflower seed to a pulp. Place one in each finger of the gloves and one in each shoe. Ceremoniously slip your hands into the yellow rubber gloves and put on your shoes. Imagine yourself stealthy and devoid of fingerprints. You do not want to leave a trace of yourself behind in this spell.

According to the lore of Solomon the king, one needed to place a heliotrope flower in the shoe or hand to become invisible. Heliotrope is a sacred solar flower named after the sun god Helios. The Greeks defined heliotrope as any flower that followed the sun; therefore sunflower or sunflower seeds are a legitimate substitute for the rare heliotrope. Yellow is the color of the sun. Gloves are a modern magical way to conceal. They are also a form of protection. Rubber is tough, impermeable, designed for electrical resistance; therefore it can neutralize any electricity this so-and-so imagines exists between you. After putting on your gloves, write this person's name on a piece of paper and immerse it in a bowl of hydrogen peroxide. H_2O_2 is a bleaching agent and a great magical neutralizer. With your gloved hands, rub your fingers harshly across the now wet letters of this person's name. Leave it to soak until the ink is bleached out. The gloves and sunflower seeds are to make you invisible to this person. The hydrogen peroxide is used to make this person disappear from your life.

If you have done a magic spell to create feelings of love in someone and have now changed your mind about it, you must continue on with part three of this spell. The ingredients will vary depending upon the spell you have performed. If you have any remnants of the spell (such as candle wax, a ouanga bag, and so on), you must soak those items in a separate bowl filled with sea salt for three nights and chant these words three times:

> *Back back back in time*
> *Undo what was done.*
> *Reverse this spell*
> *By the power of the Sun.*

Follow up by burning a blue or gray candle to neutralize the magic. If you do not have any remnants, you must duplicate all ingredients used (apples, chocolate, chicken livers . . .). Take these fresh ingredients and soak them in a solution of salt water for nine nights. Each night you must chant the verse. Stand over the bowl and repeat the words nine times.

If you worked a spell by rubbing something onto your body or ingesting food, you must soak duplicates of those ingredients in salt water and you must also bathe in a salt-water bath each of those nine nights. If you have worked a spell by ingesting products, remember to swallow some of the bathwater. On the ninth night, burn a blue or gray candle for completion. You must time this spell so that its conclusion takes place on the dark moon. Also, you must dispose of all the ingredients as well as the rubber gloves by taking them to a proper trash receptacle outside of your home.

THE POPPET FROM HELL SPELL

Ingredients:

> **poultry lacers**
> **potato**
> **eggplant**

When I was a young witchlet, I fell madly in love with a fellow named Valentin. He was not very smart, not very nice, had an awful sense of humor, very bad complexion, even poorer bank account, and he came from a horrid family. Valentin was not at all my type, yet I found myself unable to be at peace unless I was with him. I even left a wonderful, charming, handsome, spiritual, and rich lover to spend all my days and nights with Valentin. I never understood it until seven months into the relationship. I was staying in his ghastly apartment in Staten Island (and on the verge of moving in) when I discovered the source of my love for Valentin. This revelation occurred only because of poor planning on my part. I had neglected to bring enough undergarments for the whole weekend. So, on Sunday morning, while V had gone out to get the paper and brunch, I decided to rifle through his underwear drawer and borrow a pair. I grabbed a pair of BVDs and slipped them on. As I did so, some heavy object that had been caught in the garment rolled onto the floor. I stood there in Valentin's underwear, staring at an ugly old potato with my name carved on it, a plethora of poultry lacers stuck through it, and a lock of my lovely red curls stuck into the top.

My goddess, I was completely horrified. That moment marked the end of my child-hood and cloak days.

Potatoes are a very loving and nurturing food. They are ruled by the moon. Potatoes have been used as poppets since ancient times. I don't know where he got the idea to use poultry lacers instead of pins. I guess it must have come to him at work. Valentin was a chef in a highly overrated Italian restaurant. He cooked a lot of chicken and veal stuffed with various assorted things. I noticed that the poultry lacers were sharp and pointed on one end and had rounded tips on the other end. Valentin had many of the rounded tips linked together, and I realized he was using the power of the circle to keep us united. The potato was covered in lacers, but he had coupled the heads of the pins stuck through the head, heart, genitals, and feet. Each of these four sets was interlocked. Oh, did I neglect to mention that he had carved a girl figure on the potato surface? Valentin was not much of an artist, either.

I began to pull out all the pins, and as I did so, my hatred for Valentin grew and grew. I knew I needed to neutralize the spell as well as undo it. If a love spell is merely pulled apart, the subject will begin to feel hate instead of love. Once the spell is neutralized, the subject's feelings will return to a neutral state. I plopped the potato and all the lacers into his prized salt-water fish tank (I was careful not to hurt the fish). I grabbed my bag, threw on my dress, and hightailed it out of there. As I got on the ferry, I realized I was still wearing Valentin's underwear.

By the time I got home there were already several desperate messages from V on my answering machine. The following day I saw him lurking around my build-ing. For the next several weeks he followed me around. I knew I had to take ac-tion. I bought an eggplant. Sacred to Hecate and Oya, the cemetery goddess, eggplants represent death and endings. I decided to fight poultry lacer with poultry lacer. I went to the market and bought eighty-one (nine times nine) poultry lacers. Nine is the number of completion. I liked the packaging the lacers came in. "EASY>QUICK>NEAT>SANITARY" was written across the cardboard box. I waited until nine days before the dark moon to begin my spell. On the day I began, the moon was in Capricorn—best moon to get rid of a stalker. I carved the name

"Valentin" into the eggplant. I wrapped the eggplant in his underwear, as it was the only magical link I had to him. I stuck nine poultry lacers right through the cotton into the eggplant. (Cotton, by the way, is very good for delivering messages.) By the third day, the moon was in Aquarius. I focused on being free of this stalker as I stuck in the lacers. On the fifth day, the moon was in Pisces. I asked for Valentin's illusions about me to be broken. The following evening the moon was in Aries. Aries rules the head. Nine pins to quickly get the message through his thick skull. "It's over, Valentin. It's over, Valentin," I repeated nine times.

On the seventh night, I had a date with someone new. Valentin followed us around on our date. The moon was in Taurus by the eighth night, and I visualized Valentin's jealousy ending. On the ninth night, the moon was in Gemini. I traced "Dear Valentin, it's over" nine times with each poultry lacer before I stuck them into the poppet. I think he got the message. Interesting to note that on that day, his obsessive phone calls stopped. It's been nine years and I haven't heard a peep! (Knock wood.)

LOVE CURES

THE "LOVE SUCKS; I KNOW NOTHING ABOUT LOVE" SPELL

Ingredients:

milk
shot of rum
an egg
teaspoon of sugar
spritz of lemon juice

This spell is for those damaged souls who have been through the mill in love. They have failed, and they have failed miserably. They are not even willing to take another chance on love because they feel crippled underneath the baggage they are already carrying. This spell combines a bit of wisdom with a bit of hope and a whopping heap of renewal energy. This spell may be performed only on the new moon. You can perform this spell on yourself or do it for that dark and dismal friend of yours before you try to fix him or her up on a blind date.

My aunt Ruth (a fine witch in her own right) gave me this recipe. She calls it a *guggula muggula* and recommends using it for anything that ails ya. Ah, spurned one, do not despair! The goddess says in her charge: "Whenever you have any need of anything come unto me." You need comfort, consolation; to rest in the bosom of the

Lady and be renewed by her milk of divine kindness. Then you need to pick yourself up, dust yourself off, and get back in the saddle. Ride into a new romance that will hopefully take you happily ever after into the sunset. You need some milk, some rum, some sugar, a spritz of lemon, and a raw egg. Yeah, I know it sounds awful, but it will cure what ails ya.

Heat up the milk, add a shot of rum (or imitation rum flavoring), crack an egg, and stir it in (sans the shell). Add a teaspoon of sugar and a spritz of lemon juice. Take off the stove before it reaches a boil and guzzle down quickly. Lemon heals, neutralizes, and repels negative situations and hopelessness. Milk is loving and nurturing, cures depression, and alleviates fear. Rum clears the way and brings insight, eggs are for rebirth, and the sugar will sweeten the new path of love that awaits you.

SPELL TO ALLEVIATE LONELINESS

Ingredients:

shark fin soup

Shark fin soup is the surefire cure for loneliness. Stare into the bowl. Allow some tears of loneliness to fall into the soup. Stir them counterclockwise to turn their direction from sorrow to joy. Say:

*Thou art my master, but my happiness does not rest with Thee. It is through those holy ones who are part of the earthly world, and who are powerful therein, that all my desires are fulfilled.**

*Psalms 16:2–3.

*Proclaim the praise of the Lord's mighty acts from the earth, species of fish
    and all swirling floods**
Those who sow in tears will reap in exultation.**

Smile into the soup. Enjoy your own company for one solitary moment. That is the first step in attracting good company. Become your own good company. Look at your smile reflected in the soup and stir clockwise. Imagine the smile of another greeting your own. Eat the soup. Sharks have the power to cure loneliness. Witches wear a shark's tooth to ward off loneliness.

I hope you can find shark fin soup in your supermarket. I have found it in New York at a farmers' market. You can always find shark fin soup on Grant Avenue in San Francisco. You should also be able to find it in any upscale Chinese restaurant in your area. If you cannot find shark fin soup, you may substitute New England clam chowder. Clams are nothing like sharks, but they do have the ability to close themselves up in their shells and also the capability to be pried out of their shells. Clam chowder is best for those who are lonely because they are shy. Shark fin soup is more for the creature who is social by nature but somehow finds him/herself alone.

For added power, drop some flatware on the floor. It is believed that if utensils drop, company will arrive. Spoons deliver girls. Forks deliver guys. Knives remove toes.

*Psalms 148:7.
**Psalms 126:5.

HEIDI'S LOVE STALK

Ingredients:

> **three pounds apples and rhubarb (two pounds apple/one pound rhubarb)**
> **eight tablespoons of maple syrup**
> **six tablespoons of butter or soy margarine**
> **one cup flour**
> **half cup rolled oats**
> **half cup yellow cornmeal**
> **quarter cup water or apple juice (optional)**
> **vanilla ice cream**

Chop up three pounds of medium apples and rhubarb. Put them in a baking dish. Add four tablespoons of maple syrup. In a bowl, combine six tablespoons of butter or soy margarine, four more tablespoons of maple syrup, one cup flour, a half cup rolled oats, and a half cup of cornmeal. Use clean hands to mix ingredients. Continue to mix until you have the texture of wet sand. Place this mixture on top of the apples and rhubarb in the baking dish. Add a quarter cup of water or apple juice in the bottom of the pan to make it extra juicy. Place in oven and bake at 350 degrees for about an hour. Serve with vanilla ice cream.

The combination of apples and rhubarb can encourage love within a family. (Rhubarb and apple is for emotional love. Rhubarb and strawberry is used to promote sexual love. See "Red Hot Love Stalk Spell.") Because every part of the rhubarb is poisonous except for the red stalks, it is a good food to use in a *deadly* family situation—for example, when a separation or divorce is about to occur. Heidi's Love Stalk can be used to salvage the love and respect among all members of the family during difficult (and very often poisonous) times of change. Maple syrup draws sweetness forth and blessings. Maple is also good for communication. Butter is a comfort food that can soothe and alleviate fears (especially in children). Flour purifies and removes negative energy. Oats are a grain of prosperity and can help the family stay in touch with the riches (spiritual or material) that still exist among all. It can also invoke the prosperity principle so that no one starts to freak out about who is going to get what. Cornmeal is still used in many Native American rites for purification and blessings. Corn is one of the most spiritual and protective foods. In this case it is included to protect all parties and also offered in gratitude for all the positive things that have been shared together. The cornmeal is in essence a prayer asking to preserve as much good as possible in a troubled family.

Vanilla ice cream increases the appetite for love as well as for life. Usually vanilla is a sexual stimulant, but because we combine it with cornmeal, oats, and butter, its sexual effects are toned down and it becomes a "happy" food. Serve this dish to all family members.

HEARTBREAKER UNHEXING SPELL

Ingredients:

carnations
roses
sea salt
bay leaves
lemon
baking soda

If you are a heartbreaker, rest assured that you need an unhexing. Accept the fact that your dumpee(s) has placed numerous hexes and curses upon you and probably has a facsimile of your genitals in the freezer at this very moment. Please relax. Fix yourself a vodka martini with three olives and calm down before you let your imagination run wild. Now run the bathwater. Time to remove those nasty hexes. Add three fistfuls of baking soda to the bath to remove that nasty stench emanating from your heart. It's important to accept that you are the bad guy. No way around it. Now add three fistfuls of sea salt for penance and purification. Sins are meant to be absolved. Add three fresh roses and three fresh white carnations. Now you can forgive yourself and begin to love yourself again. Squeeze the juice of a lemon over the tub to help your ex get over his/her bitterness and forgive you as well. Add three bay leaves for protection just in case that last bit doesn't work right off. Now climb in the tub and soak. Soak away your sins and regain your sainthood. Remain in the tub for ten to thirteen minutes. Climb out and wrap yourself in a white towel. Get dressed and walk or drive to the closest body of water. The bathtub does not count. You must go to a river, ocean, lake, or canal. When you get there, turn around counterclockwise nine times and slap your hands together nine times. Throw nine pennies over your shoulder into the water and then walk away. Do not look back. Go home and get a good night's sleep. In the morning you'll be ready to go out and break some more hearts!

SPELL TO ALLEVIATE BOREDOM

Ingredients:

  plums

Sacred to that fun-loving god Bacchus, plums can be used to alleviate boredom. Place in a dish on a nightstand next to your bed. You can also put a plum pit under your mattress to liven up things in the bedroom. Eating plums with a partner can create more spontaneity. Eating them on your own in conjuction with doing a love attraction spell can attract a new lover who is sure to excite you and pique your interest.

KALE SPELL

I cannot begin to describe the mystical properties of kale. Sacred to Min, the Egyptian god of reproduction, it can be eaten as a fertility food. However, if eaten on a dark moon, it can banish sexual misconduct. Eaten on a new moon, kale brings prosperity to a relationship. Min was a complex god. He operated in mysterious ways. Therefore it is good to eat kale when you are not exactly sure what the problem is in your relationship. It can relieve insecurity. It can bring insight. Steamed kale can calm the nerves. Worcestershire (or soy) sauce and kale can help you solve money problems between you and your partner. Add garlic and ginger to improve your relationship in the bedroom. Since kale is also ruled by the moon, Neptune, and the sign of Pisces, if you and your partner eat it together with either fish or eggs on a full moon, you can become each other's fantasy lovers.

SPELL FOR A PEACEFUL PARTING

Ingredients:

    cinnamon powder
    curry powder
    oregano
    sage

This is a simple spell to perform when you know it's time to move on, yet your relationship has become a creature of habit. You will need a powder made of cinnamon, curry, and oregano. This combination helps to break bonds. Cinnamon will promote positive change quickly, curry will actually cause separation, and oregano will make it peaceful. You may also add some sage if the sexual or emotional bonds seem too strong to break away easily. I have counseled many couples who are unhappy in their relationship, who are definitely going in opposite directions in life yet still seem to gravitate toward one another.

You must be able to accept that it is time to let go in order to perform this ritual. It is best to have both parties present and dust each other down with the powder while you attempt to have closure. If this is not feasible, one or the other partner may dust themselves to strengthen the resolutions they have made. An excellent blend to use for abused or battered partners who keep coming back against their better judgment.

SPELL FOR FORGETTING PAST WRONGDOINGS, OR HOW TO CHECK YOUR OLD BAGGAGE BEFORE GETTING ON THE LOVE BOAT

Vus geven is geven is nisht du. *

—Yiddish saying

Ingredients:

your lover's lips

According to Hebrew legend, when we are in the womb, we retain the memory of all our previous lives. Just as we are about to be born, a special angel puts his finger over our top lip and says, "Shh." The angel makes us forget all we know and allows us to reenter the world as an innocent. The proof of this tale is found in the cleft of our upper lip. This is the fingerprint of the angel.

Sometimes relationships get too bogged down with the baggage of the past. Wouldn't it be grand to have a fresh start in your relationship? The next time your

*What is past is past, is no more.

mate digs up an old blunder of yours, try this spell instead of getting defensive or defeatist about the situation. It seems to have worked for my friends Omar and Olivia. They used to quarrel constantly and get into the "he said, she said" frame of mind. Olivia was constantly bringing up the fact that Omar was late. Omar said he may have been late a few times, but that was nothing compared to how often Olivia burned the dinner. She couldn't cook. He couldn't show up. One miraculous night he got home early, and she prepared the perfect lemon chicken. Did they rejoice in the newness of this night; did either one of them stop to ask, "Why is this night different from all other nights"? No. Omar and Olivia sat on opposite ends of the dining table and kept a silent vigil, each in anticipation of the other making a wrong move. What could have been a perfect evening turned out to be marred by the memory of past mistakes.

Only one good thing came out of that night. After dinner, Omar was reading a book and he came across the *bubbe mayse** about the lip pressing angel of lethe. The next evening, when Olivia reminded Omar of an old hurt, instead of trying to top her, he simply pinched her upper lip between his forefinger and thumb and said: "Shh-ugar." For added good measure, he drew her to him and bit her upper lip, then he gently massaged the cleft of her upper lip with the underside of his tongue. Olivia quickly forgot all the nasty things she was about to say and bit his upper lip back. She ran her tongue up and down his cleft. Apparently they have repeated this ritual several times. They tell me it led to some very interesting and refreshing activities. Angel that I am, I'll discreetly pass over *that* information and let you rediscover it for yourselves.

*Old wives' tale.

BIBLIOGRAPHY

Akerley, Ben Edward. *The X-Rated Bible.* Austin, Texas: American Atheist Press, 1984.

Blum, Ralph H. *The Book of Runes.* New York: St. Martin's Press, 1993.

Boyce, Charles. *Shakespeare A to Z.* New York: A Roundtable Press Book, 1990.

Chia, Mantak and Maneewan. *Healing Love Through the Tao.* New York: Healing Tao Books, 1986.

Crowley, Aleister. *777.* York Beach, Maine: Samuel Weiser, Inc., 1996.

Cunningham, Scott. *The Magic in Food.* St. Paul, Minn: Llewellyn Pub., 1990.

Davidson, Gustav. *A Dictionary of Angels.* New York: The Free Press, 1971.

De Claremont, Lewis. *Legends of Incense, Herb & Oil Magic.* Arlington, Texas: Dorene Publishing Co., 1966.

D'Olivet, Fabre. *The Hebraic Tongue Restored.* New York: Samuel Weiser, Inc., 1976.

Fielding, William J. *Strange Customs of Courtship and Marriage.* New York: Permabooks, 1949.

Fierz-David, Linda. *Women's Dionysian Initiation.* Dallas, Texas: Spring Publishing Inc., 1988.

Gibran, Kahlil. *The Prophet.* New York: Alfred A. Knopf, 1989 (13th printing).

Guirand, Felix (ed.). *New Larousse Encyclopedia of Mythology.* Hong Kong: Hamlyn Publishing Group Ltd., 1972.

Hand, Wayland D., Anna Cassetta, and Sondra B. Theiderman (eds.). *Popular Beliefs and Superstitions: A Compendium of American Folklore.* Boston: G. K. Hall, 1981.

Hirsch, Rabbi Samson Raphael. *The Psalms Translation and Commentary.* Jerusalem-New York: Samson Raphael Hirsch Publications Society, 1972.

Koltuv, Barbara Black. *The Book of Lilith.* York Beach, Maine: Nicolas-Hays, Inc., 1986.

Leach, Maria (ed.). *Funk & Wagnall's Standard Dictionary of Folklore, Mythology, and Legend*. San Francisco: Harper & Row, 1984.

Martinié, Louis, and Sallie Ann Glassman. *The New Orleans Voodoo Tarot*. Rochester, Vermont: Destiny Books, 1992.

Meyer, Marvin, and Richard Smith (eds.). *Ancient Christian Magic*. San Francisco: HarperCollins Publishing, 1994.

The Norton *Anthology of English Literature*. 4th ed. Vol. 2. New York and London: W. W. Norton & Co., 1970.

Panati, Charles. *Panati's Extraordinary Origins of Everyday Things*. New York: Harper & Row, 1987.

Riva, Anna. *Golden Secrets of Mystic Oils*. Los Angeles, Calif.: International Imports, 1990.

———. *The Modern Herbal Spellbook*. Los Angeles, Calif.: International Imports, 1974.

Rose, Donna. *The Magic of Herbs*. Hialeah, Fa.: Mi-World Pub. Co., 1978.

———. *The Magic of Oils*. Hialeah, Fla.: Mi-World Pub. Co., 1978.

Rose, H. J. *A Handbook of Greek Mythology*. New York: Penguin Books, 1991.

Sams, Jamie, and David Carson. *Medicine Cards*. Santa Fe, N. Mex.: Bear & Co., 1988.

Shakespeare, William. *The Complete Works of William Shakespeare*. New York: Avenel Books, *MCMLXXV*.

Slater, Herman (ed.). *Magical Formulary*. New York: Magickal Childe Pub. Inc., 1981.

Walker, Barbara. *Woman's Encyclopedia of Myths and Secrets*. San Francisco: Harper & Row, 1983.

———. *Woman's Encyclopedia of Symbols and Sacred Objects*. San Francisco: HarperCollins Publishing, 1988.

Wedeck, Harry, and Wade Baskin. *Dictionary of Pagan Religions*. New Jersey: Citadel Press, 1973.